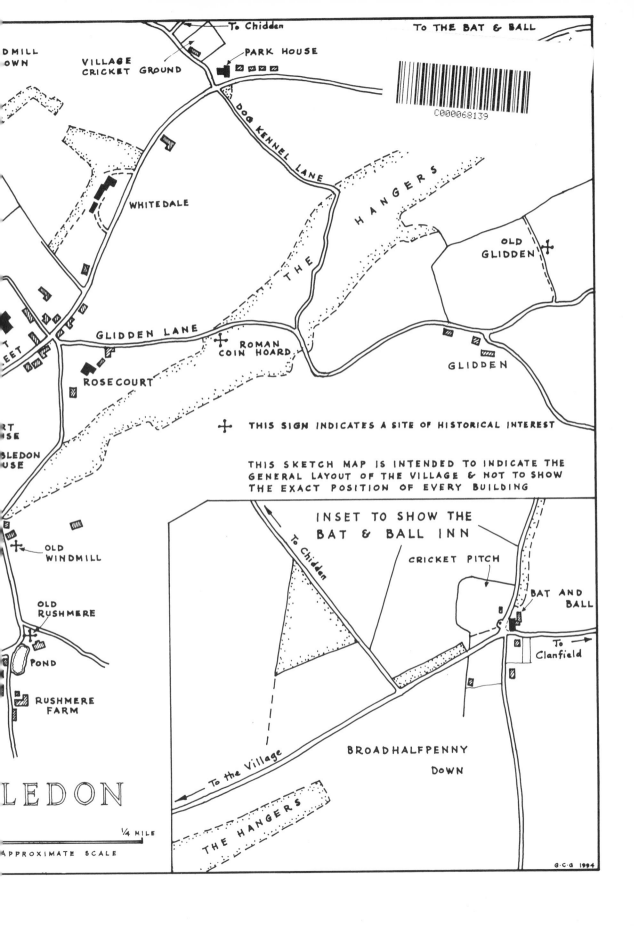

HAMBLEDON

Hambledon from Speltham Down in 1994.

HAMBLEDON

The Biography of a Hampshire Village

John Goldsmith

Phillimore

1994

Published by
PHILLIMORE & CO. LTD.,
Shopwyke Manor Barn, Chichester, Sussex

ISBN 0 85033 921 9

Printed in Great Britain by
BIDDLES LTD.,
Guildford, Surrey

For Brigid
and
Victoria, John and Philippa

1 Hambledon from the wood above Rose Court (Croft), 1994.

2 The Cricket Commemorative Stone on Broadhalfpenny Down. It was completed in 1908 by the stonemasons of Vokes and Beck at a cost of £92. The firm is still operating from Stockbridge Road under the direction of Mr. Beck's grandson.

Contents

List of Illustrations

Frontispiece: Hambledon from Speltham Down, 1994

The plates are reproduced by kind permission of the following: Major General Hew Butler, 22; Mr. Walter Quiney, 5, 21, 45, and 52; The Marylebone Cricket Club, 29, 30; *Southern Daily Echo*, 32; Mrs. Hazel Bird, 42 and 44; the Scott Polar Institute, 47; Portsmouth and Sunderland newpapers and Mr. Geoffrey Hartridge, 49; the Hampshire Fire and Rescue Service, 51; the remainder of the photographs—2-4, 7, 9, 10, 13, 15, 17-20, 24-28, 31, 34-36, 38-40, 43, 48 and 50—come from the Mrs. Kay Chamberlain's collection. The 1994 photographs (frontispiece, 1, 6, 8, 11, 12, 14, 16, 23, 41) were taken by the author. Plates 33 and 46 come from family albums.

The endpaper maps were drawn by Mr. G.C. Grant.

The pen and ink sketches are reproduced from drawings made by Dora Goldsmith, the author's great-aunt, about the year 1866, and first published in her short history of Hambledon in 1908.

The sketch in oils of the old yew tree on page viii is by the author.

Acknowledgements

Nearly a quarter of a century ago the first edition of *Hambledon* was born, and I remember with gratitude the great help, the interest, encouragement and special knowledge of my wife, my mother, General S.S. Butler of Bury Lodge and the archaeologists Michael and Mary Gough. In addition I am grateful to Desmond Eagar, then the President of the Hambledon Cricket Club and Secretary of the Hampshire Club, for allowing me to browse amongst his considerable collection of cricket books.

I am also indebted to Miss Nina Butler, Mrs. Colin Madden, Mrs. Barbara Dyer and Mrs. Pam Cullingham for permission to use their own words in the telling of the four rather unusual tales towards the end of Hambledon's story and to Mr. G. C. Grant for drawing the map of Hambledon. My spelling has always been on the original rather than accurate side, and I am grateful to Mr. Arthur Hitchins and my wife for keeping a check on this. Between us one bad spelling mistake survived to publication, and I have to say that only two people were rude enough to point it out—my brothers, William and David.

***

The invaluable help of Commander and Mrs. Betton Roberts in the launching of the first edition of *Hambledon* is detailed in the Introduction. In this second edition I am once again indebted to the Roberts family. Their son, Kenneth, and Connie, his wife, carried out a great deal of research within the village. Kenneth was particularly concerned with recording the architectural features of the older houses, while Connie was more interested in the people who lived in them. I am grateful to her for the information about some of the named people in the earlier chapters.

If anyone knows the value of carthorses, 'smaller horses', oxen, hogs, 'little pigs' and 'very little pigs' it must by Paul Heiney. His experience with horses, a hand plough and ripe manure on his traditional farm in Suffolk is well known to readers of his books and his 'Farmer's Diary' column in *The Times*. He kindly supplied the 1990s values of the items listed in the 1323 survey of Hambledon. For other matters agricultural I would like to thank Stuart Mason of the Manor Farm and the extended Crossley family who live to points north, south and west of Rushmere Pond.

There are in East Street a number of houses whose deeds go back, in some cases, to the 16th century. In 1993 we formed a small 'Deeds Group' to study them. The old papers of a single house are usually pretty boring to all but the owners, but the deeds of a line of houses spring some fascinating surprises. It was through Dot Greenwood and others in this group that we have so much information about the great fire of 1726, which swept through this area.

Joy Sang has been the greatly respected headteacher at Hambledon School since 1985. I am grateful to her for directing my attention to the school's early registers, one of which is the source of the tragic story of the diphtheria epidemic of 1883. My thanks, too, to Kath Graham and Hazel Bird, both great-nieces of Mary Ventham, for the loan of Mary's delightful diary of the 1890s.

Ronald Knight of Weymouth, Dorset, has published a number of small volumes entitled *Hambledon's Cricket Glory* into which, with his kind permission, I have freely dipped. My thanks are also due to Mrs. White and Mrs. Cook of the Records Office at Winchester.

I am also indebted to the Hampshire Assistant Surveyor, Mike Rolfe, and Assistant Chief Officer Alan House of the Hampshire Fire and Rescue Service for their help in recording accurately the story of the extraordinary floods in 1994.

Every family has its magpies and none more so than the Lunns who, in the late 1800s, started to collect postcards and photographs of Hambledon. This collection passed to their daughter and son-in-law, Ida and Ron Barrett. After Ron's untimely death through cancer, Ida gave the pictures to their son Colin, who lost no opportunity in collecting more and more of these old photographs and postcards, building up a sizeable and valuable collection. Colin was a very talented cricketer who captained a successful Hambledon

3.   Tea-dance at Ye Olde Folly Tea Gardens, 1925.

team for many years. Sadly, in 1991, at the age of 46 he suffered a fatal heart attack while playing in a match. The collection then passed to his daughter, Kay Chamberlain, and it is to her that I am grateful for permission to use so many of her interesting pictures.

I am also grateful to Geoffrey Hartridge for details of the early days of the Alliance Brewery and to other 'elders' of the village, especially Ida Barrett, Ena Brown (née Lott) and Ben Marsh, and to Robert Cecil, an established author, for his advice and encouragement. It was Robert who suggested that Mr. Hugh Peskett of Winchester might be able to help with the conundrum posed by the first toast of the Hambledon Club, ordered in 1781. Indeed I am grateful to Mr. Peskett for his very interesting proposition given in Chapter Ten.

I received many letters after the first edition of *Hambledon* had made its tentative way from this village, seeking in further continents cricket aficionados and men and women whose forebears or who themselves had once lived in and loved this valley. They contributed a wealth of new detail. In particular I would like to thank Sean Dawes of Belair, South Australia, who suggested the answer to the long-standing riddle of the Hambledon Club's fifth toast, and to thank Mr. Dawes, Mrs. W. Vincent and Mr. Paul Twynham of New South Wales and Mrs. E.M. Clay of Hambledon for the story of 'Hambledon Cottage', Paramatta, New South Wales.

In his two lavishly illustrated books on Denmead and Hambledon, Terry Norman has already used some illustrations from Kay Chamberlain's collection. I am grateful to Mr. Norman for permission to make use of his research in describing some of the illustrations in this book. My thanks too are due to Miss Jenny Streeter, Keeper of the Oates Memorial Library and Museum, Selborne.

Lastly I must express my deep gratitude to Brigid, my wife, for her great help, her suggestions chapter by chapter, her work on the index and above all for her patience.

4. The *Bat and Ball Inn*, *c*.1903.

Foreword

Trying to unravel the exact and true origins of cricket is one of the great medieval mysteries, with much of the answer lying in and around the village now known as Hambledon.

It was the Hambledon team of the late 18th century that 'raised cricket from a sport to an art', in an era when the local team was more than a match for any All England team, and when it seemed that the *Bat and Ball Inn*, run by the legendary Richard Nyren, was the centre of the cricketing universe.

Those with cricket foremost in their minds might already have read *The Cricketers of my Time* by Richard's son John, a chronicle of that golden age, but such readers will be able to discover from John Goldsmith's book so much more about the development of Hambledon as a village from early references to the community ruled by the thegn Aethelgarde in 956 and known as Hamelanduna, through its existence as a market town in the mid-1600s, by when it was called Hamuldon, and through to the present day, when cricket is still played on Broadhalfpenny Down, though Nyren and Barber's booths have been superceded by a restaurant which is attached to the historic *Bat and Ball Inn*, and which for some extraordinary reason the owners have felt compelled to call *Natterjacks*.

John Goldsmith treats his subject with all the affection one would expect from a man whose family goes back many generations in association with the village, and the spirit of the village and its past comes out strongly in this book, almost literally when the various ghosts supposed still to haunt certain houses are given quizzical mention!

England has many a rural setting that might compare notes with Hambledon through its history, and every village has its stories. Hambledon, for instance, will not be alone in having aided the young king, Charles II, in his escape to France, from where he would return to eventually bring to an end Cromwell's Commonwealth. However, the story of the exiled king's night as the incognito guest of one Thomas Symons will take some beating, and the cottage where the king slept remains to this day, now known as 'King's Rest'.

I have my own tenuous link to Hambledon through one of my more high-ranking ancestors, Admiral Sir Erasmus Gower, whose portrait, if only a small one, hangs in my study today, and who lived at The Hermitage in the early 19th century, at least when he was not out organising His Majesty's fleets.

Family link or no family link, cricketer or not, it is a delight and an education to meander through this history of Hambledon. I might be one of the first to have that pleasure, but I hope I am far from the last.

Hampshire, 1994

DAVID GOWER

The back of Churchdose Hambledon

Introduction

I started my first book about the Hampshire village of Hambledon when I was ten. It launched almost directly into the locally well-known story of the Murder Stone in all its gruesome detail, embellished with tit-bits of my own for good measure. But the furious enthusiasm with which this work was begun soon spent itself, and those still-born pages now lie forgotten in an attic.

After this my ambition to become a Great Author subsided, and I set my heart on the Royal Navy. I thought little more about Hambledon until my 18th birthday, when my mother gave me an entirely unexpected letter. On the sealed envelope was written:

John Goldsmith Esq.
To be given to him on his eighteenth birthday.

I looked at the bold, firm writing in utter astonishment, for it was unmistakably that of my father, who had died just over seven years before, while serving in H.M.S. *Hawkins*. My mother had always kept the memory of my father very much alive, and my brothers, William and David, and I knew well his two prevailing passions—the family and Hambledon. For nearly eight hundred years the family have lived within twenty miles of Hambledon, and for five hundred years we have lived in or within five miles of the village.

My father's letter was dated the 1st November 1927, All Saints' Day, and began:

My dearest John,

When you read this I shan't be alive, but I shall be watching for and hoping for your success in life and your happiness—and I wish I could have been by you to help you more practically.

Do all in your power for your mother always—she has done so much for you.

I hope in your spare moments you will love Hambledon as I have done; for more than seven hundred and fifty years, father to son, we have lived in or close to it ...

The letter ended:

... I'm sorry I haven't been able to do more for you, but it leaves you the more to achieve for yourself which is better.

Be happy and content.
Lastly, love England—always.

Your very loving Father

E. Goldsmith.

1

It was the phrase, 'I hope in your spare moments you will love Hambledon ...' that caught my attention then and that recurred most frequently in later years, running through my mind at the strangest moments. I began to be more aware of my home village and more aware too of my family's long association with Hambledon. I started, rather haphazardly, to gather notes and information about the parish's past, jotting down snippets of fact as they came my way and a mass of lore and legend.

Nearly twenty years later, in 1960, Mrs. Violet Roberts of Hambledon precipitated matters by asking me outright why I was not writing a book about the village, and before I could reply, she handed me two large notebooks belonging to her late husband, adding, 'Borrow these; I'm sure they'll help.'

When Commander Betton Roberts (known to us as Uncle Button) retired from the Navy, he devoted the rest of his life to research on Hambledon in the archives at Winchester, Southampton, the British Museum and elsewhere, carefully documenting all he discovered. To say, 'But I can't write,' when presented with half a lifetime's research, seemed churlish in the extreme.

I took the notebooks away, studied them and wrote innumerable letters to experts in various fields, most of whom were kind enough to reply. Then, with considerable misgivings about my literary ability, I began the task of weaving this miscellany of information into the pattern of Hambledon's story. Happily a small army of kind relations and friends were sufficiently interested in the project to want to help by reading, criticising, correcting and advising. They are far too numerous for all to be mentioned; it would take another book to do so. However, I must acknowledge that without 'Uncle Button's' notes this book might never have been attempted at all. So it was that the first edition of *Hambledon* was born in October 1971.

To my surprise and delight I received many letters from all over the world. There are, I discovered, little pockets of Hambledon in Zimbabwe, Australia and Canada, and other letters from India, New Zealand and nearer home all contained new and interesting information which has been included in this revised and enlarged edition.

I am most grateful to David Gower for his encouragement and interest in this edition and, despite the pressure of his many commitments, for finding the time to read the

5 The Murder Stone. This marks the spot where James Stares was brutally murdered shortly after midnight on Wednesday 21 August 1782.

manuscript and write the Foreword to this 'Biography of a Village'. Apart from the obvious link of cricket he has a family tie with Hambledon in Erasmus Gower of The Hermitage, whose unusual story is recorded in the penultimate chapter.

Here then is the story of a village, covering in various degrees of detail a community of people who, for 3,000 years, have chosen a small valley in the South Downs of Hampshire in which to make their home.

With one exception all the named people mentioned in the pages that follow were real people, and I have endeavoured to be as factually accurate about them, their characters and their achievements as possible. The one exception, the Plowman family, is imagined. Tom we will meet in the 14th century, and his descendant, William, three centuries later. Both are representative of the men who lived in the village in their own times. Their thoughts and their actions, the events and the people they describe or recall are strictly based on fact.

JOHN GOLDSMITH

Little Symonds
Hambledon
Hampshire
August 1994

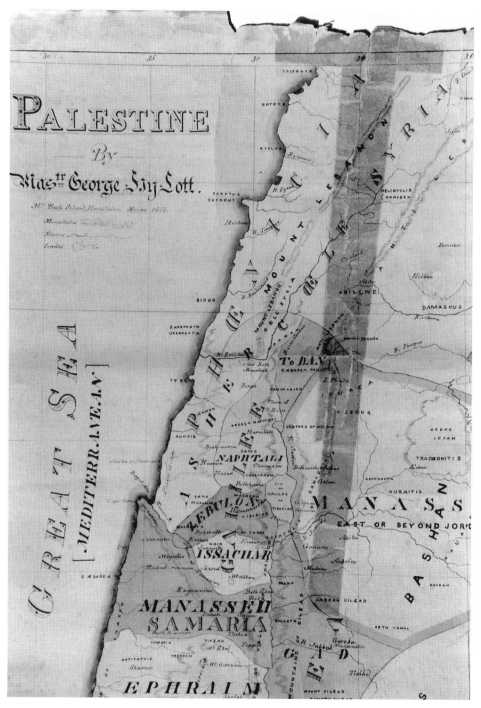

6 Detail from a remarkable map of Palestine drawn by Harry Lott in 1883 when he was 11 years old. Harry Lott's father, one of Hambledon's blacksmiths, had not sent his son to the National School but to Mr. Best's School for the Sons of Gentlemen in the High Street. (*See* page 8.)

Hambledon from Speltham Hill.

Chapter One

The Heritage

English villages appear to drowse through the summer and to sleep through the winter—unchanging, peaceful and quiet. It is part of their charm. But, as any farmer will tell you (and they never tire of doing so), crops have to be sown, harvested, gathered in and sold. Cows have to be fed and milked, pigs cared for and marketed, and the lambs, whose antics in February and March delight everyone, have to be brought to the shearing pen and finally to your dining tables. Beneath a village's sleepy charm all this work goes on as it has for hundreds of years. Methods have changed; the ox and the threshing flails of antiquity have given way by degrees to the tractor and the combine harvester. Today agronomists stalk the land pontificating about chemicals, floods of paper sweep into farm offices and colourful fields of linseed and rape punctuate the traditional areas of corn. Most of the descendants of the villein, who was once little more than part of his over-lord's livestock, now commute to the nearest town or city in their cars.

Hambledon, in Hampshire, lies amid downs hung with woods (known locally as 'hangers'), spinneys and copses 14 miles from Winchester and 12 from Portsmouth. Despite the grasping hands of this latter, ever-spreading city, which has encircled, strangled and absorbed so many less fortunate rural communities, Hambledon has managed to retain its status as a village. To the casual observer it appears typical of many Hampshire villages with its wooded downs sheltering mellow houses, old inns and a parish church which has dominated the scene for nine centuries. But for all its drowsy appearance, it is a village which has seen famous people in its streets, which has been the scene of stirring events. Kings and bishops, Cavaliers and Roundheads, murderers and world-famous cricketers have strutted their hour upon its stage and then departed. It is a village whose story may, with justification, be called unique.

Before plunging back through the centuries to the beginning of this story let us first glance at this Hampshire village as it stands today, the heritage of our predecessors, who made and lived its history.

Visiting Hambledon from the south, you would come through Denmead, once a Saxon settlement and later part of the Hambledon Hundred (though now it is a separate

5

parish and sprouting red-brick houses at the rate that mushrooms used to appear in its fields in the autumn), or you would cut through the village of Southwick and, using the smaller, winding road, pass Ervills with its concentration of Bronze Age barrows.

These two roads meet three quarters of a mile from the village centre by a Georgian farmhouse called Hook Vinney standing, with one remaining barn, beneath the fringe of a hanger which runs along behind it. It was at Hook Vinney that, in 1800, the first pack of the Hambledon Hunt was kept by Mr. Thomas Butler. The Butler family now live on the other side of the road, to the right as one faces towards the village centre. Of their large flint-built house, Bury Lodge, with its pillared verandah, we shall hear more later. Sufficient to say now that it stands back from the road in its own park, close to the site of a Roman villa.

If we put ourselves in the place of a visitor moving slowly towards the village, there lies to the right Bury Lodge park and to our left (next to Hook Vinney) Chestnut Meadow, so called on account of two enormous chestnut trees, which have stood for years in its centre. A quarter of a century ago, when I was preparing the first edition of *Hambledon*, they were truly magnificent. Today they stand with a certain aura of past grandeur, for they are beginning to show their age.

Behind Chestnut Meadow run the hangers known as Madam's Copse and Goldsmith Plantation, the latter being named after my great-great-great-great-grandfather's younger brother James, who bought it in 1752. These hangers, particularly Madam's Copse, are eye-catching at any time, but in late September, October and November they are positively spectacular. Nearly all the trees are beeches, and they fly their autumn colours from pale green through all the ranges of yellow, brown, russet and deep red as no other trees are able. They harbour a few wild cherry trees, and in the spring—the cherry trees in blossom and the beeches bursting with their bright new green leaves—they stand on an ever-changing carpet of primroses, wood anemones, dog's-mercury and bluebells. So I wrote 25 years ago, and so it was, but in October 1987 an extraordinary storm swept across the south of England leaving a trail of devastation in its wake. It cut a great swathe through Madam's Copse, and high winds in early 1988 felled other trees weakened by the earlier gale. Sadly these trees have not (by 1994) been replaced; where the woodland canopy has gone, brambles and nettles have taken over the floor once carpeted by spring flowers.

Goldsmith Plantation was cut down in 1982 and scant attention has been paid to it since; consequently saplings are struggling up through an unsightly jungle. Although neither hanger has been properly tended over the last few decades, the remaining trees still manage to catch the eye as you drive down Well Hill into the village.

But to return to the road. Below Bury Lodge stands a long, low cottage called King's Rest, where Charles II spent a fugitive night on 13 October 1651, before sailing for France. The King's host, a certain Thomas Symons, was out when the royal party unexpectedly arrived at his house. He returned later, so full of ale that not only did he fail to recognise the King (who was disguised) but actually mistook him for a hated Roundhead.

Just beyond King's Rest a lane turns off to the right beneath an arch of trees to Bury Lodge and on to Rushmere Farm. Up to the turn of the century (19th to 20th) a rather magnificent Tudor farmhouse stood to the north-east of Rushmere pond. It is strange that a house of this size and age could vanish so completely, not only physically from the site where it stood, but also from human memory. It was not until the late Colin Barrett produced a picture of this building from his unique collection of old photographs and postcards, that anyone in the village—apart from the owners of Rushmere—had any knowledge of its existence. The photograph, dating from the late 1800s, shows the building in a neglected state. There is no evidence or record of there having been a fire, so we are left with the conclusion that the old house was allowed to deteriorate to such a degree that it was finally abandoned and allowed to fall down. Tiles, timber, bricks and stones must have been removed and used elsewhere, for by the early 1900s no trace of the old building remained. The owners converted the three cottages to the south of the pond into the new farmhouse and moved in. From Rushmere a veritable network of lanes runs between fields and spinneys to other farms.

Back to the main road. Beyond the entrance to Bury Lodge Lane stands Snowdrop Cottage, fronted by a small garden where every spring a white mantle of snowdrops delights all Hambledon. Opposite we come to Cams Corner, where Cams Lane enters the main road. Lott's ironmongery shop and store stands on this corner. It was one of those delightful old shops that used to sell everything from a baby's bottle to a back axle—if only they could find it. Today the shop is in other hands, selling groceries, hardware and pet foods and providing refreshments and teas throughout the year. It is now one of but

7 The old farmhouse at Rushmere. This picture dates from some time betweeen 1880 and 1890, when the building was already in a dilapidated state. By the early 1900s all traces of the house had vanished. Its complete disappearance from view and memory is something of a mystery.

three shops left in the village. I remember old Harry Lott, the father of the present owner. When I was a boy he used to look to me rather like an Old Testament prophet even when striding purposefully towards the *Vine Inn* of an evening. His walk was upright, his face finely carved and a band of silver hair encircled an otherwise shiny, bald head (though one did not often see him with his hat removed). He had not gone to the village school; instead his father, who was one of the village blacksmiths, sent him to Mr. Best's School for the Sons of Gentlemen, which was situated at the top of the High Street, on the west side, next to the churchyard gate. Here, in 1883 at the age of 11, he produced a most beautifully executed map of Palestine and the following year an equally astonishing illuminated Lord's Prayer. And what was the end product of this special education? Harry would frequently regale his favoured customers with the answer. He left school full of grand ideas in the field of draughtsmanship only to be met by his father's 'Come on Harry,' indicating a horse in the smithy, 'get that shoe off.'

Cams Lane leads up past a mixture of some very old and a few rather newer cottages to one of the loveliest houses in Hambledon—charming, sequestered, Jacobean Cams. This house, perhaps more than any other in the village, is pervaded by an atmosphere of the past, and of its ghostly voices more will be told later. At Cams another lane, branching off to the left, runs back through Goldsmith Plantation and

8 The Lord's Prayer penned by Harry Lott when he was 12 years old. This and the map of Palestine on page 4 are the two illustrations I really regret not being able to present in colour.

Madam's Copse, while the main lane passes out of the parish near the Murder Stone on its way to Hoe Cross and the neighbouring village of Soberton.

Next to Lott's Store, on the main road, runs a row of four modern houses, one of which has an atom-bomb shelter beneath it. The one next to Lott's, Anvil Cottage, was converted from Hambledon's last smithy. Opposite this row of houses stands a Victorian flint-built house called Quarry Wood, with cottages on either side. The one at the far end was once a sweet shop. This was a great attraction for the pennies of myself and my brothers (in the days when 1d. would secure eight king-size gobstoppers), for my parents' house, The Cottage, stood opposite. This house, like others in the village, might appear to be a Queen Anne house with its parapeted front—but this was a later addition disguising extensions to a three-storey Tudor cottage. Alas, half the garden has been sold off to a developer. One can only wait and see what will appear in a once much-loved garden.

Moving on again towards the village we pass, on the right, a small estate of council houses, called Barn Crescent after a 200-year-old barn which was pulled down to make room for it. Opposite is Hartridge's mineral waters factory. Beer used to be made here as well as mineral waters and soft drinks, but in the Second World War a German bomb scored a direct hit on the building (luckily causing no casualties) and the brewery side was never rebuilt.

Beyond Hartridge's and Barn Crescent there is a cluster of houses, including some old timbered cottages, around the area where the road forks. The right-hand fork, which

9 West Street in Victorian times, leading to the village centre. On the left, Green Lane leads to Droxford and the Meon Valley. The *Green Man Inn*, now a private house, stood behind the photographer.

10 The *Green Man Inn* c.1908. Green Lane is on the right and the footpath taken by James Stares and John Taylor (*see* Chapter Eight) leads away to the left of the inn.

we will presently take, leads on to the centre of the village, while the left-hand fork leads to Droxford and the Meon Valley, and is known as Green Lane. Right up to modern times it was no more than a lane, but in the early years of the 20th century Droxford acquired a railway station, and houses sprang up along its length for some one and half miles. The lane had to be widened and resurfaced to accommodate the increased number of coaches and carriages which then used it and, although Droxford station was closed long before the era of Dr. Beeching's axe, Green Lane is now the major road. On the western side a number of houses lie under the shelter of Litheys Hanger and on the east there are more houses, the Ebenezer Chapel and another council estate called Stewart's Green, beyond which are some flats, bungalows and small houses built under the Housing Association's Affordable Housing scheme. It bears the name of Lashly Meadow in memory of one of Hambledon's greater sons.

At the corner where Green Lane meets the village road, there stood the *Green Man Inn*, but this lost its licence in 1951 and the old pub was converted into a private house. Opposite, on the village side of the corner, is Harfield, where my wife was born. Moving on towards the centre of the village, we pass on the left Harfield's old grounds which ran along behind a low flint wall. Parcels of this land have been sold off and, at the time of writing, new houses are beginning to appear. Next we reach the rather cleverly designed Village Hall, which was built in 1982, and the Youth Clubhouse, both on what was once Harfield's land. Beyond them is the *Vine Inn*, one of Hambledon's four remaining pubs, which dates back to the 16th century. On the right-hand side of the road, opposite Harfield's wall, are some houses, one of which contains a painted beam, dating it to between 1590 and 1600. Further on we come to Orchard House, which was once a brewery before Hartridge's time, and Vernon House which used to contain the manual telephone exchange. What a difference from today's six or ten digit numbers! Well after the last war, no one in Hambledon who had a telephone possessed more than a two digit number. You would pick up the receiver and ask for, say, '23 please.' You might well hear Freda May at the exchange inform you that the person you were calling was having tea with Mrs. So-and-So and 'Shall I put you through there? Oh, and did you know that Mrs. White's baby arrived at three o'clock this morning? A boy—eight and three quarter pounds ...'

Next to Vernon House is the great brick and concrete eyesore that used to house the Southdown buses which plied between Portsmouth and Hambledon. Hartridge's have now taken over this edifice and use it as a store, and a small bus company, based elsewhere, provides a regular service between the village and Portsmouth. Opposite the old bus depot are some more houses including my own, Little Symonds, named after the meadow in which it was built. These lead on to some very pleasant retirement bungalows. Once, when I was there admiring the attractive gardens which front them, open conflict was narrowly averted between a veteran of Mons and a veteran of Gallipoli as to who had had the 'better war'!

Then comes the *New Inn,* built as a coaching inn towards the end of the 17th or early 18th century. It was here that, one Wednesday evening in August 1782, the ill-starred meeting of two men occurred which led to violence, tragedy and grim retribution. A lane turns off to the left past the inn and the area behind it where its stables and coach houses used to stand. In the late 1950s they were rat-infested and rotten, and crying out for a small fortune to restore them; instead they were pulled down and the area cleared to accommodate a small meeting hall and a parking place for the less romantic but more practical vehicles of the present day. Beyond this car park there are a number of houses including two thatched cottages and the spacious Old Vicarage with its William and Mary façade, added some time after 1841 to replace a Georgian front which itself completed considerable extensions to a Tudor core.

Opposite this lane, on the other side of the main road, is the Manor Farm House, parts of which date back to about 1200, and whose 16th-century additions were once decried by a passing visitor as 'There's a bit of mock Tudor for you!' From Manor Farm a terrace of old houses, which includes the post office and Clark's Stores (The People's Market), leads into the very heart of the village. On the opposite side of the road other houses lead to the Copper Kettle, once a café but now a private house. The main road runs in a roughly west-east direction. To the north, or left as we enter the area, the High Street runs steeply up to the church, the oldest parts of which have dominated the village for over 900 years, but its great 13th-century additions have made it far larger than Hambledon's modern population requires (the population in 1971 was 1,700; in 1991 it was 870).

The High Street is, perhaps, the oldest highway in the village. Up its sharp incline to the church have walked Saxon and Norman, serf, villein and feudal overlord, copyhold tenant and freehold tenant, peasant, yeoman, squire and knight. It was also, in 1726, the scene of a disastrous fire. At the churchyard gate the High Street turns abruptly to the east and changes its name to Church Lane. It is lined with houses, some of which must have been rebuilt or extensively repaired after the 1726 fire. Church Lane then turns to the north past The Folly, erected in Victorian times by a farmer who wished to build a tower which commanded a view of his entire domain. At the village school, Church Lane becomes Hogs Lane and runs on past the modern vicarage to join the Droxford road (Green Lane) or on past West End to Chidden.

Opposite the High Street, Speltham Lane leaves the main road to the south-east, and winds up past Speltham Down. In 1984 these rolling fields were due to be sold as one piece of land or in lots. An appeal was launched and by public subscription the whole down was bought by the village and passed on to the National Trust. It is now one of the few chalk downs owned by the Trust. The wild flowers are a delight. Cowslips are followed by carpets of buttercups with clover and ox-eye daisies galore, then the orchids—Common Spotted, Bee, Pyramidal, Common Twayblade and Greater Butterfly—bud and bloom in their turn. Speltham Lane continues up one of the steepest parts of the downs, giving to the houses here superb views of the valley village, as it climbs towards Rushmere and the network of lanes beyond. Where the lane leaves the main road there stands the *George Inn*. Here the old Cricket Club held its annual dinners in the 18th century, the Hambledon Hunt Balls were held in the 19th century and from here the coach left to catch the Portsmouth to London stage-coach near Petersfield.

Anyone living in the village who enters this 'square' formed by Clark's Stores, the Copper Kettle, the post office and the *George*, where the pulse of Hambledon beats, even with the avowed intent of quickly purchasing one simple item—a pound of cheddar, a book of stamps or a glass of beer—is unlikely to leave it again in less than half an hour. During that time he or she will have met what might seem like half the village, and have been brought right up to date with 'village news'.

Continuing along the main road, with the heart of the village now behind us, we pass, on the left, what may appear to be a series of Georgian houses, but most of them were built in the early 16th century and acquired Georgian fronts when repaired or rebuilt after the fire of 1726. The Hambledon Garage with its showroom was here but this sadly closed in 1993. Opposite, behind its wall and trees is Hambledon House, and a little further on more houses line the road until we come to the Court House on the right. This has had so many alterations and additions through the years that no one knows how long its oldest portions have stood, nor how long ago it was first the site of the manor court. Beneath it the old court dungeons or cells still exist. Beyond, more houses line the road until we come to the entrance of the lovely Regency house called Fairfield, which is thought to stand in the field where one of Hambledon's two fairs used to be held. Beyond Fairfield a lane runs up on the left to Mill Down where, in 1951, Sir Guy and Lady Salisbury-Jones, with great family enterprise, planted a vineyard. It is in other hands now. Opposite Mill Down Lane there are two houses which once served as the poorhouse. Beyond these, two other lanes lead off the main road through

11   The heart of the village, 1994. Compare with the same view in 1900 on page 92.

hangers, straddling a large, flint house called Rose Court. One of these leads to Glidden and passes close to the spot where a hoard of Roman coins was found. There are a few houses around Rose Court and from them the main road emerges into the country proper, passing Whitedale House on the left and Deepdale (once Whitedale Farm cottages) on the right. Then on to Park House, which is partly Elizabethan and contains a 'priest's hide' in the thickness of one of its walls. Here a lane turns off to the left past the modern cricket ground to West End and Saxon Chidden, while on the right Dogkennel Lane leaves the main road to join the network of lanes to the south and east of the village.

For about one and a half miles the main road winds and climbs through fields and downs, the view becoming magnificent. At the top of the hill, on the very perimeter of the parish, lies that hallowed plot of land—Broadhalfpenny Down, the nursery ground of English cricket. It is a bleak spot swept by wind and rain in winter, and in summer it stands in isolation before the *Bat and Ball Inn* amid rolling Hampshire country. In the past I have played there many times and have always been impressed by the number of visitors—cricketers, spectators and tourists—who remark on the extraordinary way in which one feels the atmosphere of the past. It is not difficult to imagine the thronging, expectant crowds that came to watch 'Little Hambledon pitted against All England' in the 18th century. It is not difficult to imagine the players—the furious bowling of Brett, the 'provokingly deceitful' bowling of Richard Nyren, the unequalled batsmanship of John Small, and also the Duke of Dorset and Lord Tankerville, both as colourful on the field as off it amid all the bright trappings of nobility they brought with them. One can almost hear the happy carousal that would always end a day's cricket, for, after the stumps were drawn and the pitch surrendered to the long evening shadows, the day would close with wine and song—the inseparable companions to Hambledon cricket.

> Then fill up your glass, he's the best that drinks most.
> Here's the Hambledon Club—Who refuses the toast?

Having now a little knowledge of Hambledon as it is today, we may slide back through time to the beginning of its story. This starts in the dimming mists of 5,000 years ago with Stone and Bronze Age burial grounds, and continues through an Iron Age fort to a Roman villa. It is taken up by a church which tells of Saxon, Norman and later periods, and all the while it is coloured in its passage through time by charters, deeds and wills, lore and legend till it is brought to its climax in Hambledon's moment of glory on Broadhalfpenny Down. A solitary stone in the hedgerow of a lonely lane weaves in the black thread of murder, a communal grave in the churchyard tells of a disaster and the war memorial of sacrifice.

Our forebears have left much behind them through which we are able to glimpse their fluctuating fortunes which have brought to Hambledon prosperity and contentment, hardship and bitterness, brief greatness and decline on the tides of time gone by.

Old Cottage in Green Lane Hambledon.

Old English barrows to the left of Farcham Road. Hambledon.

Chapter Two

Hamelanduna

Six thousand years ago the valley we now call Hambledon was submerged in deep forest. Whether or not primitive man of the Old Stone Age hunted the animals that lived there we cannot be sure. It is said that a hand axe of the period was found in the parish, but the proof is missing—no one today knows where it is.

About 3500 B.C. the art of domesticating animals and sowing corn gradually spread over England. Slowly the New Stone Age dawned, having taken nearly 5,000 years to reach these islands from the Near East, and in their everlasting battle for existence men learned to depend less and less on hunting wild animals and more on the art of farming.

Hambledon's first farmers built rectangular wooden huts on the downs surrounding the valley, and round their settlements they cleared small plots of land and sowed wheat and barley. But more important than their crops were the herds of cattle, on which they depended, together with their goats, pigs and sheep.

The New Stone Age people fashioned their own pottery and were highly skilled at making bone and flint instruments. Their axes were very different from those of the earlier age. They had a smooth finish and were fitted into handles; these were the main tools used for the great work of land clearance. The New Stone Age people generally buried their dead in long barrows, great mounds of earth anything from 30 to over 100 ft. in length. One such barrow remains near the village today.

In about 1850 B.C. bands of settlers began to arrive from the continent with a knowledge of metals, and by 1700 B.C. Britain entered the Bronze Age, nearly 2,000 years after it had dawned in the Near East. Farming techniques developed, the standard of pottery improved, life was no longer such a desperate struggle for existence. Like his Stone Age predecessors, the Bronze Age man was deeply religious, though we have not yet discovered what gods he worshipped nor how he worshipped them, but it was during the late Stone Age and early Bronze Age that the world-famous temples of Avebury and Stonehenge were built.

In contrast with the New Stone Age people, Bronze Age man buried his dead in round barrows, more than fifteen of which may be seen today on the downs which surround Hambledon. It is strange that the only real evidence of Hambledon's early farmers comes to us through their deaths and burial grounds, for little evidence of their lives has been found. Their weapons, tools, axes, knives, needles, necklaces and lucky amulets of stone, bone and bronze must lie in profusion beneath Hambledon's fields, downs and hangers.

For many generations Bronze Age communities wrested their livelihood in the Hampshire valleys, living peaceably together. For the most part they were unmoved by the ceaseless comings and goings, infiltrations and minor invasions of the people generally known as the Celts. The story of the coming of these warlike people is complex in the extreme and scholars do not all agree.

Undoubtedly there was a complicated series of migrations and minor conquests, the best known being that of the Gaels who came about 750 B.C. They sailed by the western sea routes directly to Ireland, the Isle of Man and Scotland, where the Gaelic is still spoken. Then between 600 and 500 B.C. the Brythons, who gave Britain her name, spread through the south-east of the land, though they are now mostly represented in Wales.

It was not until about 500 B.C. that, crossing from the north coast of France to the Hampshire harbours, the Celts arrived in force. They brought with them goods made of iron, thus heralding the Iron Age in Britain, and they also brought with them a military age. The peace that had prevailed for so long between the scattered agricultural settlements in the downs and valleys of Hampshire gave way to organised raids and tribal warfare. The tribes thereafter kept themselves separated from each other by deep zones of forest and fortified hilltops.

It was on the summit of a hill known today as Old Winchester Hill, which is about three and a half miles from the village of Hambledon, that the Celts built one of their hill-forts in the traditional manner of the fifth century B.C. The old single-line rampart around the contour of the hill can be seen clearly today, and there are no signs of complex defences at the entrance, which were a feature of the forts built later in the Iron Age. There used to be a dew pond among some trees and scrub close by, but during the Second World War it was wired off and has now grown into a small, thick jungle of scrub, shrub, bramble and wayside weed. But even so, in the heat of summer and drought it is always damp and marsh-like in its centre.

The manner in which these ponds retain their water, even during prolonged droughts and despite their use by cattle and sheep as a drinking source, has long been a mystery. The name 'dew pond' misleads one into thinking that the dew at night keeps them replenished, but this cannot be true. The draining of water and even the condensation of mist on nearby trees and shrubs are more likely factors.

From 500 B.C., as year followed year and century followed century, peace and with it prosperity and order are believed to have returned to Hampshire. Records are not plentiful and authorities are inclined to disagree, but it does appear that, despite the example of the warring tribes of Dorset and Wiltshire which were forever fighting among themselves, Hampshire settled down to administer itself and build roads between its townships.

There are few records of the Roman invasion of Hampshire. In A.D. 43 Titus Flavius Vespasianus (who later became Emperor of Rome) was 34 years old and in command of the Second Legion. With it he subdued the Isle of Wight, and then swept through Hampshire without serious opposition, the speed and ease of his passage probably accounting for the lack of records. However, the county submitted to new masters and new administrators, remaining under them for three and a half centuries—a period comparable with the entire history of the United States of America since the sailing of the *Mayflower*.

Peace was not long in returning to Hampshire. The Romans divided the country areas into estates called villas, and towards the end of the first century a thoroughly Romanised Briton found himself vassal to Rome but overlord of a villa in the fields and woodland of what is now Hambledon. He lived to the south of the present-day village in a house with walls two feet six inches thick, built of large, shaped flints and mortar. Some of the rooms were lined with square red tiles and the building was roofed with tiles of a lighter red.

Immediately in front of the house there were probably flower beds—perhaps of roses—and beyond, fields of corn and pasture spread to the edge of the great forests. The landowner might be seen riding about the estate in long leather boots, and with a short cloak over his tunic. He spoke Latin as well as his native Celtic dialect and had probably taken a Latin name.

Hambledon prospered under the Roman way of life. The whole of southern Britain became a civilisation of unfortified country houses, and its people grew soft and quite untrained in the art of war or of defending themselves, and therefore, from about A.D.370, they began to fall easy prey to Saxon raiders. Soon after 382 a certain Romano-Briton, living to the north-east of the present day village, buried his savings in fear of these raids, but he never came back to collect them. Elsewhere about the villa perhaps others did the same.

As the century drew towards its closing years the power of the Roman Empire steadily waned. In the south the raids of the Angles, Saxons and Jutes continued and increased, while the Roman army, already diluted with Saxon mercenaries, was vanishing to fight even more desperate wars on the continent. It was probably in these last years of the fourth century that the villa of Hambledon was destroyed and its people killed, scattered or enslaved. In 410 when, it is said, the last active Roman soldier left Britain, a curtain of chaos, that was not to be lifted for more than two centuries, fell about the beleaguered province.

Slowly mother earth covered the wounds made in her surface by the ruins of Roman Hambledon. Lush grass, waving corn, bushes and trees grew where once a proud Briton with a Latin name lived with his family and slaves; all trace and thought of them were utterly lost and forgotten.

Fourteen centuries later, in 1800, Mr. Thomas Butler bought a house called Bury Lodge, which stood on the road to the south of the village, just where the lane turns off to Rushmere. It was in such bad condition that he had it pulled down and rebuilt further back from the road. While the foundations of the new Bury Lodge were being dug the workmen discovered a coffer of Roman coins, but this unexpected find was not properly reported; both the coffer and the coins 'disappeared'. The only reference we have of them now is a rather sad passage in a letter of Thomas Butler's referring to their 'disappearance'. Even with this clue no further thought was given to Roman Hambledon; it was only in the light of what was later discovered that we now wonder how close those workmen's spades came to disclosing some other evidence of Hambledon's Roman days.

Not long after the Butler family moved into the new Bury Lodge, they discovered, on a bank behind the house, broken pieces of earthenware, a few red stone tiles and part of 'an old wall'. Nearly a century later these remains were recognised as Roman, and in September 1910 six men dug the area for nine days. Almost at once they found walls about a foot high and two feet six inches in width, built of large, shaped flints held in mortar. To the north-east, in a corner, there were traces of fire, a quantity of ashes and pieces of melted glass. Also found were some deer antlers, nails, bones and a great many fragments of pottery. These were later classified as New Forest ware and the imported highly-glazed brick-red and black pottery known as Samian ware. There were also some local Celtic fragments and pieces of locally made imitations of New Forest and Samian ware. This tells us little save that the owner of this villa at least ate off and possessed some good pottery.

Scattered round were the remains of the red tiles which once roofed the building, and the tiles with which (according to the excavators) the walls had been lined internally. Five coins were also found, two of which were dated as mid-fourth century.

In those nine days less than half of what was described in the report as a 'court-yard' was cleared. From the reports and drawings available today one can be certain of only one thing; whatever was discovered was not a 'courtyard'. It was more likely to have been part of the villa house itself, but only re-excavation properly conducted could establish or disprove this. Today there is nothing visible except a slight ridge where the diggings were made. Mother earth has once again spread her mantle over her scars and, almost certainly, over other secrets this short-lived enthusiasm missed.

Now and again, by chance, corners of this mantle are lifted, as in the case of the man who, sometime after A.D. 382, buried his savings in fear of Saxon raids. What became of him or his family we shall never know. He may have perished at the hands of the Saxons or fled the area. He never returned to retrieve his savings, which amounted to at least thirty-three copper coins. They were found nearly 1,600 years after their burial by Mr. George Booth of Hambledon while he was enjoying a walk in the hanger a little to the south of the lane that leads from Rose Court to Glidden. The earliest of the 33 coins found was a 'Constantinopolis' dating from about 330, when Constantine founded his new Rome on the Bosphorus, and the latest was struck in the Emperor Gratian's time, probably about 382.

In 1943 a spade sliced into a skeleton buried about three and half feet below the surface in chalk. It was not an archaeologist's spade that unearthed this Roman find, but that of a soldier digging an air-raid trench about 400 yards south of Bury Lodge.

Once again the matter was not properly reported. The trench was completed and the bones offered to a dog, which somewhat naturally was not amused. They were finally handed to the Denmead police constable, Hambledon's policeman being away at the time, and were subsequently identified as being Romano-British. A later search revealed nothing but a few scraps of rusty iron, the largest of which was one inch across and appears to have been the head of a nail or stud.

To return to the unhappy, violent and turbulent years that followed the departure of the Romans—the early years of the fifth century and the beginning of the Saxon era. That part of Hampshire between the river Meon and the Sussex border, which includes Hambledon, is thought to have become predominantly Jutish, and Hambledon became part of the Meonwara—the people of the Meon. The Jutes have left behind them no trace or records of their life in Hambledon. The Roman villa, the church (if one existed), and all that had been built up in Roman times were laid waste. Even Christianity, which first came to Britain in the later period of Roman rule, was submerged in the waves of the Anglo-Saxon conquest.

About the year 650, nearly sixty years after Saint Augustine landed in Kent, that stormy petrel of Christianity, Saint Wilfred of York, was shipwrecked off the south coast and discovered the benighted state of the Meonwara. He returned with missionaries to reconvert the people and build churches once more in the towns and villages around. These churches were built of logs bolted together in an upright position, and it is possible that one existed in Hambledon. Village legend says that such a church stood on or near the site of the present church, but there is no evidence to support or refute this.

It is not until 956 that we hear of Hambledon again, and then we discover the village has a name. In that year King Edgar granted ten hides at Chidden to his thegn (a somewhat nebulous Saxon rank of nobility, less than an earl) Aethelgarde. This would amount to about 1,200 acres of arable land with wood and wasteland in addition. Some of the boundaries given in the charter recording this grant can only be guessed at today—for example: 'along the brooks [of the people of Chidden] on to the ruined house.' Others, though, are quite clear even now, as 'along the dene to the westernmost barrows.' A final boundary refers to 'the cultivated lands of "Hamelanduna",' which is the first recorded form of Hambledon. There is no doubt that these boundaries correspond with the modern tything of Chidden, about 2,000 acres, and now part of the parish of Hambledon. They include roughly the whole of the parish which lies north of Chidden Holt, probably including the Holt itself but not the northern part of Broadhalfpenny Down.

Hambledon's modern name evolved slowly from the Hamelanduna of the Chidden charter of 956. In the 1094 will of Athelston Aethling we find Hamelandune, but in Domesday Book the name is shortened to Hamledune and Ambledune. In the 13th- and 14th-century charters the 'don' first appears—Hameldon and Hameledon, and in the 14th and 15th centuries we find Hameldon and Hamuldon. The name Hambledon first appears in an indenture dated 1611 and in the Bishop of Winchester's Fine Book from 1636.

Generation upon generation of Hambledonians have discussed the origin of the name of their village and, of the many possible derivations, the two following appear to give the most satisfactory answers. The first and most likely stems from 'ham', the Saxon for homestead, and 'duna', a down or hill—thus 'the homestead in the downs'. However, Hamela might have been the name of an early settler, and as 'n' is the Saxon genitive termination, Hamelan would mean Hamela's. If we think of Hamela as a Jute settler whose down bears his name to this day, 'Hamela's Down' is a second and rather attractive possibility.

About a century after Aethelgarde acquired Chidden, a stone church was built at Hambledon in the 'Saxon style' and this forms the oldest part of the present day village church. It has stood, a silent witness to more than 900 years of the village's story. But let us leave Hamelanduna now, in the closing days of the Saxon era, a Christian village belonging to the Priory of Saint Swithun of Winchester.

Chapter Three

Quill and Parchment

In 1066 the fields of Hamelanduna were ploughed, sown and reaped. The harvest had been gathered into the granaries, and the trees were touched with the first tints of autumn when news of King Harold's defeat at Hastings percolated to the manor. The tremendous significance of this single battle was quite lost on the ordinary men and women who toiled in Hambledon's fields and who were now preparing for the winter.

But for loyal Saxon landowners the news spelt disaster. From the battlefield at Hastings Alwin returned to his home in Hambledon where for many years he had been overlord of an estate of about 400 acres. Twelve villeins and their families with two serfs worked the farm and looked after his cattle, crops and pigs. Six of the villeins were comparatively well-off, owning about 180 acres of land between them. Alwin also possessed a mill at which his people came to grind their corn, paying for its use with corn, eggs, honey or hens.

Submerged in the national catastrophe of defeat in war are all the lesser tragedies, which sweep over individuals and families through death and dispossession. For the serfs and villeins of Hambledon little more was required of them than to settle down to the different ways of new masters—but for the landowners like Alwin disaster was complete. They lost everything they possessed and, worse still, they left their native villages knowing that hated Normans were to live in their houses, attended by their servants, enjoying everything they had built up over the years. In such manner did Alwin and his family leave Hambledon.

Another small estate was owned by Edward. Like Alwin he was a Saxon but, as Edward had not supported Harold at Hastings, he had been allowed to retain his land. It was only about 200 acres, and two serfs worked the farm which contained much woodland. But even for Edward life could never be the same. He was now a despised Saxon in a Norman land—even his serfs probably despised him.

In 1070 William the Conqueror seized all church lands. Hambledon, with the great manor of East Meon, passed from the overlordship of the Bishop of Winchester into the hands of the Crown and nearly a century was to pass before its return.

A few years later a number of men on horseback rode into the village. The clatter of the horses' hooves on the hard mud road below the church was scarcely stilled before they demanded the bailiff and the king's steward, who was holding Hambledon on behalf of the Crown. Some women and children and a few old men gathered around; the horsemen, it seemed, were about the king's business.

The king's steward came forward, greeted the strangers and arranged for the horses to be taken to his stables. When the bailiff arrived, slightly out of breath, he was immediately dispatched by the leader of the group to fetch six villeins, trusty and true; the party then entered the manor house. A small crowd gathered outside, both curious and anxious—hungry for news. The bailiff returned with the villeins, who were showered with questions as they disappeared into the house. The bailiff turned at the door and shouted, 'Ye bide your time and ye'll learn.'

A moan, peppered with some loud, ribald remarks, greeted this rejoinder as the door closed. The crowd did not wait long after this, for there was much to be done in the daily lives of these people; in twos and threes they drifted back to their homes or strips of land. Only a handful of young children remained and they were lost in play.

Meanwhile in the manor house the bailiff and the villeins were made to swear a solemn oath to answer questions truthfully and completely. The strangers then questioned them all closely and with quill squeaking across parchment, wrote down all they learned. Later they visited holdings within the manor such as Edward's and that of Alwin which was now owned by a Norman, William de Perci. Then, as suddenly as they came, they departed.

This visit caused great excitement and curiosity, so that more questions were showered on the chosen six. What was all the writing about? A book on the king's orders about the village? A book about all England? Impossible!

The excitement soon died down, but the amazingly detailed survey of all the lands of England, Domesday Book, was completed in 1086. It contained the following information for each holding of land of any consequence:

1.   The name of the overlord, or tenant holding it under him.
2.   The name of the person holding it in Edward the Confessor's time.
3.   At how many hides it was assessed in King Edward's time and at how many in 1086.
4.   How many ploughlands there were and how many of these were in the lord's demesne farm, and how many villeins and borderers held the rest.
5.   How many slaves there were.
6.   How many mills there were and their value.
7.   How much wood there was, expressed as wood for so many pigs.
8.   The value of the holding in King Edward's time.
9.   The value when granted by William.
10. The present value (1086).

The information was obtained on the oaths of the sheriffs, the lord of each manor, reeves of hundreds, bailiffs and six villeins of every village.

Before mentioning the entries relating to Hambledon, a brief explanation of some of the terms used may make them easier to understand.

A hide was a unit of land measurement in Saxon times, and is generally considered to have included 120 acres of arable land with pasture and wood in addition. It was retained by the Conqueror mainly as a unit of assessment for Danegeld, the tax imposed to buy off the invading Danes. William levied this tax several times at a rate of six shillings per hide, but the normal rate was two shillings. (Money then may very broadly be considered as having about 1,000 times its 1990s value, so six shillings in 1086 would be the equivalent of roughly £300 in the early 1990s.)

The ploughland was the chief unit of land measurement in the Conqueror's time. It is also believed to have included about 120 acres of arable land, which was considered to be the amount of land one plough and its team could deal with. The hide was more or less the equivalent of a ploughland, but as it came to be used more as an assessment for tax purposes so the number of hides and ploughlands ceased to correspond.

The demesne farm or lands were those which the lord of the manor kept to supply the needs of his establishment if he was resident. If he was not resident, as in Hambledon's case, his tenant or steward would account for the profits or arrange for the dispatch of the produce to the lord of the manor.

The work on the demesne lands was performed by villeins and borderers. A villein probably held about 30 acres of arable land (a virgate or yardland) in his own right, but was liable for service on the demesne farm. A borderer was also liable for service on the demesne lands, but only held a few acres of his own with his cottage.

There are only two entries in Domesday Book mentioning Hambledon by name. One concerns the land that had been granted to William de Perci and the translation reads:

> In Meonstoke Hundred, William de Perci holds Ambledune. He received it with his wife. Alwin held it from King Edward. Then as now it was assessed at one hide. The land is three ploughlands. In demesne is one; and six villeins and six borderers with two ploughlands. There are two slaves and a mill worth twelve pence. Wood for four pigs. In the time of King Edward and now it is worth £4, when received £3.

The second entry refers to a hide in Hamledune held by Edward. There was one ploughland in demesne with two borderers and wood for six pigs, and it was worth £1.

These two references to Hambledon clearly refer to only a very small portion of the parish, which has an area of more than 9,000 acres. Some authorities say that the survey of Hampshire was not completed, but this opinion has been disputed and others have said that much of Hambledon was recorded under the great manor of East Meon, which is more likely.

In the next seventy years the unchanging toil in Hambledon's fields went on as before. Rich and poor were born, were married, raised their families and made their last journey to hallowed ground. In the outside world William I lost his life on a battlefield in France, William II was shot, by accident or by design, while hunting in the New Forest, the greatness of Henry I was followed by the anarchy of Stephen and finally the even greater reign of Henry II began.

It was during this reign that Hambledon was returned to the church of Winchester. Although the charter making this grant was not dated, signatures on it narrow the time to between 1154 and 1161. This charter is of interest because it describes Hambledon's status at this time as 'an appendage' to the manor of East Meon. It reads in translation:

> Henry, King of England and Duke of Normandy and Aquitaine and Earl of Andigavia to all Archbishops, Bishops, Abbots, Earls, Barons, Justices, Viscounts and all his faithful of England and Normandy, Greetings.
>
> Know that I have given to God and to the Church of Winchester which is built in honour of God and the blessed Apostles, Peter and Paul and of St. Swithun, the Confessor, the manor of East Meon with all its churches, chapels and appendages to wit Hambledon and others of the same manor of East Meon belonging and the manor of Wargrave with all its churches, chapels and appendages, an eight days increase in the fair of Winchester, so that the fair, which in the time of King Henry, my grandfather, only lasted eight days may now last sixteen days.
>
> And this I have done for the welfare of my soul and for the welfare of the soul of King Henry, my grandfather, and of other Kings as well past as to come.
>
> Witness: Theobald Archbishop of Canterbury.
>   Hugo Roto Magister Archiepiscopus.
>   ...? Episcopus.
>   Philippus Episcopus.
>   and Reginald Earl of Cornwall.
>   and Henry of Essex Constable.
>
> At London.

At about this time Hambledon's Saxon church had stood for about a hundred years. Its nave measured 37ft. by 18ft. 6 ins. internally, and the chancel about 16ft. by 14ft. The high walls were broken at intervals by square columns partly built into them and partly projecting; these projections were later called pilaster strips. It was simple and unremarkable to the Hambledonians of that day and it looked very similar to the present-day Saxon church in the neighbouring village of Corhampton. Just to the south-east of the main entrance stood a young yew tree and it is still there today.

In the summer of 1970 two boys were smoking cigarettes in its ancient branches. Thoughtlessly they threw the lighted ends down the hollow trunk and the tinder-dry debris within its base began to smoulder; at about midnight it burst into flames. The trunk acted like a chimney and soon flames were roaring up its entire length. They were finally extinguished by the fire brigade.

For several years it was touch and go as to whether the old tree would survive or die, but survive it did thanks in large measure to two sessions of major tree-surgery and an overwhelming wave of concern generated in the village. In 1985 details of the tree and its surroundings were forwarded to the Conservation Foundation (Country Living) under the aegis of David Bellamy. This organisation recorded the age of our tree as 950 years.

Through the centuries many enlargements have been made to this simple Saxon church, each carried out in the contemporary style of architecture. This has resulted in a church of singular beauty and dignity which, to an architect, reads like a book—Saxon, Norman, Early English and Perpendicular; yet there is no clash of proportions,

12 The yew tree by the porch of Hambledon church is about 950 years old. It survived a
serious fire in its hollow trunk in 1970.

13 These Norman arches, which pierced the original Saxon external wall, date from about 1160.
The dog-tooth and rosette motif is unusual. The photograph dates from 1910.

no jarring note, but a building within which Hambledonians and visitors alike find peace and beauty.

It was about 1160 that the first enlargement took place. The north wall of the Saxon nave was pierced by two Norman arches with unusual mouldings and massive pillar shafts, and a north aisle was added from the west wall to the line of the chancel arch. About twenty years later a south aisle was added, the original south wall being pierced by two slightly pointed arches in the late Norman style, not symmetrically opposite the north arcade, and in the west walls of both aisles small Norman windows were added.

Today practically nothing of the old Saxon work is visible. The old north and south walls formed an internal arcade and were later covered in plaster. The western wall was removed in the 13th century and replaced by an arch when the tower was built. The Saxon chancel arch was replaced in the same century when the chancel was enlarged. The only Saxon work that remains uncovered today is parts of the pilaster strips, which can be seen above the Norman arches, and parts of the cornice of the original Saxon chancel.

At the time of the Norman additions there lived in or near Hambledon a certain Richard de Preesthaghe and his wife, Florence. An ancient deed in the Hampshire Record Office at Winchester infers that Richard applied to build a chantry or side chapel where his family could be buried and prayers said for their souls. The bishop's approval was not forthcoming. However, at some time before 1187 the de Preesthaghes gave their land at Edgarsham to Hambledon church and the translation of their charter reads as follows:

> Charter of land of Edgarsham given to the church of Hambledon.
>
> Know present and future men that I, Richard de Preesthaghe, and Florence, my wife, have given and granted, and by this charter have confirmed, for our souls and for the souls of our fathers and mothers and relations, to God and to the church of the blessed apostles Peter and Paul of Hambledon all our lordship which we had in Hambledon: to wit that land which is called Edgarsham with all its appurtenances to be held in free and pure and everlasting alms. And that this gift and grant may remain firm and unshaken for ever we have confirmed it by the force of the present writing and of our seals.
>
> Witnessed by William then Chaplain of Hambledon, Germanus of Ervilles, Matthew of Denmead, Jordan of Kendal, William son of Paganus, William Buret, Symore ..., Henry of Crabden, Walter Cleric, Andrew of Chidden and many others.

This charter is of interest because among the witnesses who signed it are 'William then Chaplain of Hambledon' and 'Walter Cleric'. It is through this document that the board in the church today, which lists 'The Vicars of Hambledon', is able to begin:

> Before 1187 William Chaplain
> Before 1187 Walter Cleric

In 1187 Richard Toclive, then Bishop of Winchester, gave the vicarage of Hambledon to a priest called Terricus, and his appointment was confirmed by Pope

Clement III some four years afterwards. For this living Terricus received the offerings of the altar and cemetery and all the small tithes (which excluded the tithe of corn) and a small amount of land attached to his vicarage. Life was not easy for him because there was not much money in Hambledon at this time; the village was all but self-supporting, and there was little need or use for it. However, for the benefice Terricus had to pay two marks annually to the bishop. (It is very difficult to relate the value of two marks in the 1190s to an equivalent value of the 1990s, but if you plunge into the bran tub of speculation you might come out with about £1,300.) For five years Terricus struggled to raise and pay this sum, then in 1192 or 1193 the Bishop, 'considering the benefice collated to him small and less than enough for the support of his life', reduced the pension of two marks to one besant, 'moved thereto by Divine pity'.

However Terricus was not alone in having financial difficulties at this time. Richard I succeeded his father, Henry II, in 1189, and out of the ten years of his reign he spent only seven months in England, and then only for the purpose of raising money. From the outset it was clear that his mind was set on the Crusade, and his whole policy was directed towards providing funds and making the necessary arrangements for the kingdom during his absence. Of the many measures he took to raise money one was to sell Charters of Confirmation, from which, it seems, no grant or deed was safe. It appears that Richard made the Bishop of Winchester buy such a charter, confirming Henry II's 20-year-old grant of the manors of Wargrave and East Meon with Hambledon, for three thousand pounds of silver.

Worse was to come. In 1193 England was on the brink of civil war, the situation could scarcely have been more desperate, and Richard, while returning from the Crusade, was captured and held to ransom. The sum ultimately fixed for his release was 150,000 marks, which was a huge amount for those days—double the whole revenue of the Crown—but it was raised and paid. Richard returned to England in 1194 and immediately set about raising money. It was not long before this utterly ruthless king took away once more the two manors of East Meon and Wargrave for which charters of confirmation had been bought.

In 1199 Richard's brilliant but useless life was ended by an arrow while besieging a castle in France, and on 26 December of the same year King John finally returned the manors of Wargrave and East Meon with its appendage, Hambledon, to the church of Saint Peter, Saint Paul and Saint Swithun of Winchester.

The Manor Farm
the gable end very
old probably
a chapel

Chapter Four

The Hambledon Hundred

The first Sunday in January in the year 1200 was an unusually glorious day. It was almost like spring. As the people of Hambledon emerged from the subdued light within their Saxo-Norman church, where for the last two hours they had attended Mass, they blinked in the bright sunlight outside. They gathered in little groups around the yew tree that stood by the south entrance, marvelling at the sun which shone from a clear blue sky. Although the ground around them was still as hard as iron, no trace of the early morning's frost lay upon its surface.

They wished each other a happy New Year—the manor wits, a happy new century. The exchange of greetings was much the same as it is today, but there was more sincerity in the voices of these people. When they passed among themselves the season's good wishes, the thoughts behind their words were that the year's crops would be good, that they would not fail, that none would starve. That epidemics would not sweep through the manor, cutting them down as the harvester's scythe in the cornfield. That the manor might prosper.

Men and their families from the outlying communities such as Denmead, Ervills, Teglease, Chidden, Rushmere, Glidden, Pithill and Crabdene met and exchanged news with those of the main manor of Hambledon. Slightly apart from the peasants, the lord of the manor's steward was talking earnestly to the steward of the absentee overlord of the manor farm at Denmead (called Rookwood since the 19th century), for they were both having new houses built. In another group a number of freemen and their families were discussing the trials and troubles of running the small estates they owned, the laziness of their few villeins and serfs, the value of corn and the difficulties of getting their produce to the nearest market.

Gradually the people started moving down the slope that led from the church to the centre of the village. Set along the streets were the villeins' huts. Each one had a small garden in which vegetables were grown and chickens reared. The smaller houses were simple one-roomed shacks made of mud and stones with a hole in the roof to let the smoke out. There were a few better houses made of a timbered frame with walls of mud and straw plastered onto basketwork of wattle. Roofs were thatched with straw, and floors were of earth trodden hard, through which, on rainy days, water oozed. From all these houses, large and small, the pale blue smoke of wood fires curled lazily into the clear January sky.

Most people, even those of the outlying communities, returned to their homes on foot. Some rode on their horses, but no one used a cart, for such a practice was despised as a weakness. The steward of Denmead farm paused with his friend, Matthew, the bishop's steward, at the new manor house, which stood about 250 yards south of the church. It was not yet completed and was surrounded by an untidy forest of scaffolding which looked far from safe. It was to be a two-storey house. The three foot thick walls of hewn chalk and flint had reached their full height and rising above them, poised like talons, were the first curved beams to take the roof.

'It's further on than Denmead,' grumbled the tenant of that estate. 'What a time to put up with all this! Work should have started last summer. Our present house is falling down around us.'

'You'd never get the labour in the summer,' said the bishop's steward, 'leastwise not around here.'

The conversation shifted around the usual subjects of common concern to farming tenants of great overlords, to the serious news from France, while the women chatted and their children fretted, impatient to be home. None had an inkling of the grave crisis, only eight years away, which would touch them all.

Both Rookwood, which stands just over a mile to the south of the village, and Manor Farm exist today. Neither house was large for a manor house, though both have

14   The Manor Farm. The oldest parts of this house date back to about 1200.

16th-century and modern additions, and for many centuries a great barn stood adjacent to the Manor Farm house.

In 1200 the people of Hambledon and its surrounding communities must have been aware that their country possessed great dominions across the Channel. In the next six years some, perhaps, sailed to France in the vain effort to protect them. But in Normandy fortress after fortress fell until, by 1204, the whole province was lost. In the next two years all the English possessions in northern France suffered a similar fate. If any men from Hambledon returned they must have had a sorry tale to tell, but these misfortunes were completely overshadowed by the much graver crisis at home which was to affect every man, woman and child.

The seed of this catastrophe was sown in 1205 with the death of Hubert Walter, Archbishop of Canterbury, and the need to select his successor. While the monks of Canterbury chose one candidate and King John another, Pope Innocent III, the proudest and most powerful of all the medieval popes, chose and consecrated a third without consulting John. The king, weak but arrogant, refused to submit to this outside interference with his prerogative, and the great quarrel with the papacy broke.

In 1208 the Pope laid England under an interdict. This meant that every church was closed and there could be no burials in consecrated ground, which was a terrifying blow to a religious and superstitious people. John retaliated by outlawing the clergy and seizing church property wholesale. The Pope rejoined by excommunicating the king (1209), and the churches remained closed for five years.

Terricus had been vicar of Hambledon for 19 years when these troubles began. He undoubtedly received his orders from the Bishop of Winchester, but we do not know how he interpreted them, or how he lived during those five years, whether the practice of Christianity went on underground or whether Hambledonians were left resentful and without spiritual support.

In 1213 Innocent III declared John deposed and invited the king's long-standing enemy, Philip Augustus of France, to take possession of the English throne. This not only brought the coward king to heel, but made him the abject vassal of the Pope, and Innocent's choice, Stephen Langton, who two years later was to lead the barons to the Great Council at Runnymede, where the Magna Carta was signed, became Archbishop of Canterbury.

Despite the great quarrel between King John and the Pope, life went on in the manor. In the year 1208-9 Serlo, the reeve, presented the year's accounts to Matthew, the steward of the Manor Farm on which four carters, one blacksmith, one swineherd, two shepherds and three labourers were paid a total of 23s. 9d. for the whole year.

At the manor court, Gilbert Trenchem was fined 12d. for fighting and affray; Godfrey, the smith, paid 12d. for permission of the Lord Bishop to have his daughter married and Roger Black was fined 6d. for encroaching on the highway. In the year 1210-11, Richard Cog was fined 12d. for not doing his ploughing service on the manor farm and William Asketil was also fined 12d. for searching Osbert's house without a licence. Richard King paid two shillings for permission to inherit land. Serlo, the reeve, recorded that an ash tree was cut down to make boards for the bishop's house; 32 sheep were cured of scab; corn was given to Ferando, the crossbowman, on the bishop's instructions and a windmill was dismantled at Hinton and brought to Hambledon to be reassembled.

In 1216 a capricious, unstable boy of nine became King Henry III of England. With the throne he inherited raging civil war throughout the land and the presence of the heir to the crown of France, supported by a large number of barons, holding a great part of south-east England. In the next fifty years great men rose and fell and the names of some of them may have been known dimly to the people of Hambledon as the masters and architects of their country's standing—Stephen Langton, Archbishop of Canterbury; de Burgh; Peter des Roches, the warlike Bishop of Winchester who became the king's favourite after his return from the Crusades and who virtually ruled the country for two years before his fall; Simon de Montfort and others. But more important to Hambledonians than the manoeuvres and counter-manoeuvres of the great men guiding England through these difficult years was the steady growth in importance of their village, as it approached its first great and perhaps most significant date—1256.

There came a day in that year when a messenger bearing the news reined up his horse outside the manor farm. There was nothing unusual about this, for messengers from Winchester were not uncommon. It was the speed with which the reeve was sent for that set tongues wagging and rumours flying until the news itself broke. The king, Henry III, had granted Aymer de Vallance, bishop elect of Winchester, the right of a weekly market in Hambledon to be held on Tuesdays. The people were summoned to the manor court. The terms for setting up the stalls were explained (these included the payment of a tax to the lord of the manor) and permission to set up stalls was granted to certain people and recorded in the rolls. There was still much to be done. A market place had to be established, the stalls made, the news spread to outlying communities and the tollbooth arrangements made. The rules governing markets were strict. A hut called the 'tollbooth' was always erected nearby which accommodated a small court designed to deal with infringements of rules, disputes, difficulties and the collection of the tax. It also had the power to punish offenders.

No time was lost and it was very likely on the next Tuesday after the court meeting that Hambledon's first market was held, probably at the bottom of the hill below the church. Obviously things took a little time to settle down but initial shortcomings were readily overlooked. The people of Hambledon and its surrounding communities no longer had to walk or take a cart some seven or eight miles—perhaps further—to market. To begin with the goods bartered and sold were largely home-grown produce and articles of everyday use; people bought what they had not grown themselves. Later, as the village prospered, the market became bigger and better attended, more people came bringing with them more goods or money, the range of goods widened and the village thrived. The cultivated lands of Hamelanduna of three centuries back, the appendage of the great manor of East Meon of a hundred years ago, now had the right of holding its own market. Hambledon grew rapidly in stature and in prosperity, and greater things were to follow.

There were more visits from journeying pedlars passing through the manor; friars preaching, teaching and selling indulgences brought news (very limited and outdated by our standards today) of the outside world, news of wars and rumours of wars, scandals, disasters and occasionally, let us hope, good tidings. Blacksmiths and wheelwrights set up their forges and workshops; cobblers, tanners and tailors were also drawn by the market. Inns and ale houses prospered, themselves calling on brewers, coopers and maltsters. Travelling apothecaries may have brought herbal remedies to the market. Housewives grew skilled in the use of medical herbs: agrimony was a 'comfort to them that have naughty livers', rue was an insecticide and also a tranquilliser, lungwort was suitable for chest complaints, poppy could be used as a cough syrup, foxglove for those with trembling hearts, wormwood was used as a worm expeller.

Soon after the advent of the market a vast programme of work to enlarge the church began. It is not absolutely clear in what order these alterations were carried out; there was certainly one major change of plan while the work was still in progress. However, the first step was the removal of the small Saxon chancel arch, which was opened up and replaced by an exceptionally fine arch in the Early English style, and the Saxon chancel was extended to the east. It is at this point that the order of work becomes obscure. By the end of the century a completely new chancel had been built further to the east, onto the new extension, and the Norman north and south aisles were extended to the east as far as the new chancel, the original Saxon chancel and its extension being pierced by arches of the contemporary Early English style. Many windows date from this century, and below the east windows of the north and south aisles there were altars in addition to the high altar. Also during this century a western tower was built, so that the church in the early 14th century looked much as it would today without the porch and vestry.

The glass in the windows is modern, mostly late Victorian, but it is of passing interest to observe the window portraying St Peter and St Paul, to whom the church is dedicated. The painting of Peter, with his key to the Kingdom of Heaven, is inscribed 'Paulus', while the fiery apostle of the epistles is entitled 'Patras'.

At some time before 1286 the tythings of Chidden, Glidden, Denmead and Hambledon were formed into the Hambledon Hundred. The hundred was a territorial division within a county. Its origin is obscure but has some connection with the territory sufficient to support a hundred families—or put another way—a hundred ploughlands, a ploughland being considered as the amount of land which one ox team or family could manage. However, the hundred was chiefly important at this time for its Court of Justice. Ordinary sessions were held every three weeks, and twice a year, after Easter and Michaelmas, a special sheriff's court was held in accordance with Magna Carta. Civil cases were tried by the freeholders of the hundred, all the inhabitants of the area being required to attend to declare the custom, but only the sheriff or the lord of the manor could try criminal cases.

So Hambledon grew in status, but wherever prosperity flourishes there lurks a grasping or begging hand. In 1291 Pope Nicholas imposed widespread taxation in order to raise money for the last Crusade. The benefice of Hambledon was assessed at £13 6s. 8d. and was required to pay £1 6s. 8d. tax.

From what is known of Hambledon and conditions of life in the country areas of England in the 13th century, it is possible to take a speculative look at Hambledon 700 years ago—say in the 1290s.

The lord of the manor of Hambledon was the Bishop of Winchester and he seldom set foot in the village. The manor and its demesne farm were managed on his behalf by his steward, who lived at the manor farm house and passed much of the profit and produce of the farm to Winchester. There were others who owned land in Hambledon besides the bishop. One was William de Perci, whose family had owned about 400 acres in Hambledon since William the Conqueror's time, some 220 years before, and another was Ralph de Camoys, after whose family the area of Hambledon called Cams may well have taken its name. Unlike the de Percis, who were not resident landlords, the Camoys family did live in the village and were to do so for many years to come.

The previously mentioned communities around the main manor, Chidden, Glidden, Rushmere, Denmead and Ervills to mention the main ones, were dependent on a land-owner, his tenant or even a freeman, and were managed on the same lines as the main manor farm. The arable lands of these farms were divided into three vast fields, one of which lay fallow each year. In these fields almost every serf and freeman held a number of scattered strips according to his standing.

15   The Hambledon Hunt meet at Cams *c*.1904. It is thought that the area around Cams took its name from the de Camoys family who lived in the village in the 13th century. In 1904 Captain and Mrs. Harvey lived at Cams.

The serf or villein paid for his holdings by labour. He was legally obliged to work from one to three days each week on the demesne farm and, further, he was legally bound never to leave the estate. In a sense he was his lord's property—part of the livestock of the manor, but he had his rights. He could not be discharged or sent off the manor so long as he did not fail in his responsibilities, and he had other rights guarded by the customs declared in the courts and recorded in the rolls. The freeman, who held a larger amount of land than the villein in the great fields, owed no service to the manor except attendance at court.

The manor or hundred court convened regularly about every three weeks. Almost the entire population was bound to attend to join in declaring the custom. At these courts disputes about rights, trespass and other civil matters were settled, and men were selected for special communal duties such as a reeve to act as foreman, haywards to put up fences when the crops began to grow, shepherds and swineherds for communal flocks and herds grazing in common pastures and so forth.

Beyond the great arable fields were the hay meadows in which each villager had his share. Beyond these again was wide spreading waste, mostly wooded, but where freeman and serf had certain rights of pasture that were rigidly defined, and where shepherds chosen in the court looked after the animals on behalf of their owners. The lord of the manor or his tenant had his rights too. He jealously guarded his hunting in the waste areas, and he also enjoyed other profitable perquisites such as his mill at which the peasant ground his corn, frequently in return for farm produce.

Hambledon was probably all but self-supporting. The people lived on their own crops and meat from their own cattle; they wore clothing of home-tanned leather or home-spun clothes made from the wool of their own sheep; they warmed themselves with wood taken from their own waste lands. They lived in huts made from wattles, timber and clay, each in its own small plot of land. Apart from the little luxuries wanted at the manor house there was little needed from outside the village—salt, spices to preserve meat for the winter, iron for mattocks and ploughs and possibly salted fish for use in Lent. Most of this was usually available at the Tuesday market when, except at harvest time, nearly all work on the soil would stop for the selling or bartering of grain, wool, hides, honey and other goods.

When the crops failed, the people were in real danger of starvation. They had little use for money, and knew little of the outside world except what they might gather on market day, or what might percolate to them from the manor house or some travelling friar or priest.

A great gulf, conceived as having been set by God, was fixed between landlord and serf. Apart from but approachable by both was the priest.

> God hath shapen lives three;
> Boor and knight and priest they be.

In Hambledon matters connected with the church were left in the hands of John Terri, vicar of Hambledon, whose vicarage and church provided the centre of such spiritual and intellectual life as there was.

We, on the threshold of the 21st century, are apt at first thoughts to pity the poor peasant who lived in our village seven hundred years ago, but was his life so wholly grim?

He could not be deprived of his land. He had plenty of company, for he was a member of a close-knit community, which was more powerful than we, today, might think. He lived where his grandfather and his father had lived before him, and his house would not be broken into by thieves. His world was small but intense, and it was shared. He and his neighbours shared a common pasture where a swineherd he had helped choose in the court looked after his animals. He shared a common woodland, a common meadow and a common wasteland. Though he worked hard he enjoyed many holidays, for in addition to Sundays there might be as many as 40 church holidays a year. Then he would dance, sing the ballads his parents had taught him, sit with his friends or play games. Perhaps wandering conjurors, acrobats or mountebanks with trained bears would arrive and give a performance in the village.

We have no means today by which this peasant's joys and sorrows may be measured, but since he was taught not to overvalue earthly existence, and since his experience in a world of almost unchanging custom prevented his thinking constantly of ways to improve his lot, and since, above all, there were people around him bearing the same burdens he bore—was his life so wholly grim?

Chapter Five

Bishop takes King's Pawn

Alexander, Prior of Winchester, read the letter his scribe had just brought to him and his face slowly purpled with rage. He walked over to the window and glared out across the priory cloisters towards the great Norman tower of the cathedral. It was one of the last buildings still caught by the evening sun, but nothing within the prior responded to the beauty of old Winchester as it gradually succumbed to the long evening shadows. Alexander, his face still the colour of a Lenten chasuble, wheeled round upon his scribe, but he had already fled. The prior was quite alone in his sombre, dark-panelled room.

The year was 1323. Reginald Asser, Bishop of Winchester, had just died. Indecently soon afterwards, scarcely before the late bishop's mortal remains had been laid to rest, the prior had received the letter he now held in his hand. It was from Robert de Welle, Keeper of Temporalities, reminding him that the first fruits and profits of the manors of Hambledon and East Meon reverted to the Crown during the vacancy of the See. It also contained a request that the necessary arrangements be made for the mustering of the stock and the valuation of the two manors.

Only four years before, the prior bitterly reflected, Bishop John Sandall had died, and during the year before the enthronement of the bishop-elect—now, alas, himself dead—the manors of Hambledon and East Meon had been subjected to a detailed survey. The produce and profits formally due to the bishop had been taken by the Crown Exchequer instead of reverting to him, Alexander, Prior of Winchester. His anger burned up within him anew as he recalled the late bishop's lack of interest in the matter.

Whatever his scribe's failings, and they were numerous, he was at least thorough. The prior went over to the olive wood table on which lay a small pile of parchments, and selected one headed 'Stock on Episcopal Manors—Dilapidations on the Death of Bishop John Sandall until Delivery of Temporalities to his Successor'. He took it over to the window and read by the failing light: 'Hameledone: Convictum est per Sacramentum Philippi de Demulle, Johanis de Colmere ...'

This document, a detailed survey of Hambledon, compiled on oath by a number of jurors, gives us a very good idea of the size of the manor farm and the value of the livestock and crops in those days over 670 years ago, when the great victory of Crecy was still to be won, and the ravages of the Black Death yet to be endured. Its translation reads: (For comparison the figures in brackets show the estimated value in 1990.)

Hambledon: It is shown by the oath of Philip of Denmead, John of Colmere, William Yvon, Richard le Camoys, William de la Dene, Laurence, Galfridi le Taillour, William of Chidden, Robert le Bole, John Trenchemere and Steven Martyn, Jurors,

That there remain in the aforesaid manor:

2 Cart Horses	18/-	(£2000	each)
9 Smaller Horses	price ½ Mark each	(£1000	each)
7 Oxen	at 8/- each	(£600	each)
1 Bull	5/-	(£900)	
6 Cows	at 5/- each	(£650	each)
3 Young Oxen	at 4/-	(£250	each)
4 Yearlings	at 3/-	(£200	each)
145 Wethers		(£55	each)
7 Rams		(£250	each)
242 Breeding ewes		(£60	each)
99 Lambs		(£30	each)

They say, too, 100 of the best wethers were sold by the bailiff at 1/6d. each. (£75 each)

Also there remain:

1 Boar	Price 3/-	(£150)	
3 Sows	at 2/-	(£120	each)
9 Hogs	at 1/6d	(£60	each)
26 Little pigs	at 10d	(£45	each)
9 Little pigs	at 3d	(£15	each)

They also say there remain there:

3 Carts (with iron fittings) with harness	4/- each	(£7,500)
2 Pots of brass	Price 2/6d	
1 Little pitcher	Price 10d	
2 Dishes of brass	Price 1/6d	
1 Basin with lavatory	Price 1/6d	

Dilapidations of houses assessed at £5, of the Chancel 1 Mark.

LAND SOWN: They say there are:

				per acre
Sown with wheat	51 acres	Price per acre	4/-	(£140)
Sown with barley	28 acres 2 roods	per acre	3/-	(£135)
Sown with oats	99 acres	per acre	2/-	(£120)
Sown with vetches	3 acres 1 rood	per acre	2/-	(£75)

IN GRANARY estimated

85 quarters of wheat	at 4/- a quarter	(£120 per ton)
12 quarters of Quadragesimal barley	at 2/6 a quarter	(£130 per ton)

SALE OF WOOD

Felled and sold in the Park by Robert Thorncumbe: 10 oaks price 26/- (£1,500)

A broad abstract of the above figures gives a clearer idea of the acreage of the demesne farm, what crops were grown in the great fields, what livestock worked them or grazed around them and their value.

LIVESTOCK	£	s	d	OTHER STOCK	£	s	d
11 horses	3	18	0	3 carts with harness		12	0
21 cattle	5	15	0	5 receptacles		8	10
493 sheep	c.25	0	0	1 basin with lavatory		1	6
48 pigs	2	6	5				
					1	2	4
	36	19	5				

LAND SOWN	£	s	d	IN GRANARY	£	s	d
51 acres wheat	10	4	0	Wheat	17	0	0
28 acres 2 roods of barley	4	5	6	Barley	1	10	0
99 acres of oats	9	18	0				
3 acres 1 rood of vetches		6	6		18	10	0
	24	14	0				

SALE OF WOOD	£	s	d
10 oaks felled and sold	1	6	0

The assets of the manor farm, not including any buildings, would appear to be about £82. The figures show nearly 182 acres under cultivation and there were probably about 91 acres lying fallow, which points to a total acreage of arable land of 273 acres, beyond which would lie the hay meadows, the grazing pastures, waste lands and forest.

***

Alexander, Prior of Winchester, read the letter his scribe had just brought him and his face slowly broke into a smile. He walked over to the window and stared out across the priory cloisters towards the cathedral, resplendent in the noonday sun. He turned towards his scribe, but he had left.

The year was 1330, and the message was from the bishop, John Stratford. Along the top of the parchment the bishop had written in his own hand, 'At last we have won through.' Beneath, in the immaculate quillmanship of one of the bishop's scribes, was written:

> Grant by Edward III to John, Bishop of Winchester, on his petition, which set forth that, whereas the churches of East Meon and Hambledon, being parish churches were annexed to his Bishopric as spiritualities yet on the last voidance of the See, Robert de Welle and his fellows, keepers of temporalities, intermeddled with these churches, as other keepers have in time past, by accounting the fruits thereof at the Exchequer among issues of the temporalities—in the future the keeper of the spiritualities is to deal with them and their fruits.

Alexander laid the parchment aside and thought for a moment about Hambledon, and not altogether with a clear conscience. Old John de Bourtone, who had been vicar there for nearly forty years, had written at regular intervals reminding the bishop that the work on the church had long since been completed, and the new altar had still to be consecrated. His last two letters, though respectful as ever, had a distinct edge to them. Life had not been too easy in Winchester with the two previous bishops, Sandall and Asser, both living for only three years after their enthronement (a thought that still burned into bitterness with Alexander, as it reminded him of the battle with the Keeper of Temporalities). Nevertheless, Bishop John Stratford had now been enthroned for seven years.

Alexander reflected that he would like to see Hambledon; he would talk to the bishop about the consecration of the altar and suggest that he accompany him. But in the event John Stratford never visited the manor. Before a date could be fixed for the ceremony he became ill and died. In the following year, 1334, the Register of Bishop Orton simply records: 'On the 16th day of November, Wednesday, of the year of our Lord aforesaid he dedicated to the Lord the high altar of Hambledon'.

In 1340 taxation raised bitter resentment throughout the country areas. It rose to the value of every ninth lamb, ninth fleece and ninth sheaf of corn valued as in 1291, and a jury declared the value for Hambledon as £14 13s. 4d., an increase of £1 6s. 8d. over the 1291 assessment. Eight years later the greatest catastrophe of all time, the first wave of the Great Plague, later known as the Black Death, broke over England. In 1362 it struck again and in 1369 it swept across the country for a third time. Records are scant. Some authorities say that half the population of England, then about four million people, died in the first epidemic alone, but whether this is an exaggeration or not, certainly whole villages were wiped out. How Hambledon fared during these terrible years we have no means of knowing. Along the southern boundary of the churchyard there is a bank which is said to be the communal grave of the victims of the plague. Certainly at its eastern end an ancient communal grave was discovered containing bones lying higgledy-piggledy in the disturbed earth as though they had been thrown into a pit in a haphazard manner. Just to the north of this the ancient skeletons lie in an east-west direction where they were laid to rest in ordered graves.

This came to light in 1986 when the foundations for an addition to Beechview Cottage were being dug. In medieval times the owner of that house (perhaps it was the vicarage in those days) added part of the south-east corner of the graveyard to his garden and built a wall around his ill-gotten gain. The present owners decided to use this land to add an extension to their cottage, and it was when the garden was being lowered to match the level of the new extension that the bones were discovered almost directly under the old wall. There they remain to this day, sealed in by a new garden retaining wall while flowering shrubs bloom above them.

From the accounts of the bishop's manors a strange record concerning Hambledon has come down to us. It appears to be neither complete nor consistent and its purpose is not clear, but it does indicate that Hambledon was, perhaps, more fortunate than some in the years of the Black Death. It is reproduced below, and as can be seen in the 'number of sheep' recorded there is no significant fall, and although the net balance of some unnamed account dropped £36 in the year following the first epidemic, it soon recovered.

		Number of Sheep		
	1208-9	533		
	1345-6	699		
	1347-8		net bal. £88	Church £80
first epidemic	1348-9		£86	£?2
	1349-50		£50	£69
	1351-2		£95	£57
	1353-4	987		
second	1362 and			
third epidemics	1369			
	1376-7	1,145		

Another inference that Hambledon may have weathered the plague better than sister villages may be drawn from the ploughing tables kept by the lord of the manor. These tables were strictly recorded at this time, and also included fines imposed for work not completed, or for neglect of a holding. After the plague there were references to acres of ploughing being excused at Meon and Hambledon, but in 1376 a table of 'Ploughing Services Performed' records that Hambledon ploughed 152 acres. This figure is only 30 acres short of the acreage of crops recorded in the 1320 survey of the manor during the vacancy of the See.

In the next chapter we will see how jealously guarded were the hunting and game rights of lords of manors. In 1387 there was, brought by the prior of the manor of Nursling Priory, an action against John Goldsmith of Southampton and others for infringing his fishing rights in the river Test at Nursling. They were accused of carrying off 200 lampreys, 300 salmon, 200 trout, 4,000 eels and other fish to the value of £40. The record tells us that John Goldsmith was, at this time, holding the manor of Testwood on a nine-year lease from Sir Thomas West, and that he asserted in his defence that the fishing of the Test between Ashridge in the north and Dodepoll in the south was common to the lords of Nursling Priory and Testwood and that therefore he and his servants were entitled to fish therein. The case was adjourned, but with what result we do not know. The numbers of fish in question seem staggering and unfortunately no time scale was given, but over a reasonable period of time and with the use of nets such quantities would have been quite possible.

***

On a bench outside the ale house sat old Tom Plowman*, feeling none too well. It was the morning after his 59th birthday, during which he had consumed far too much ale. The house was closed now, but the bench before it was in a warm, sunny place where an old man could sit and ruminate while his sons and grandsons worked in Hambledon's fields.

It was the summer of 1399, the last summer of the century, '... and nigh on my last summer too,' thought old Tom. He was quite the oldest member of the village, for it was not usual for a peasant to live so long, and so he sat now indulging to the full the great privilege of the old—reminiscence. Perhaps it was because there was so little time left before him that he lived so much in the past, and was always talking of the 'good old days' before the Black Death.

'Happy days then,' was his recurring theme. 'Y' can tell the way men don' sing now as they used, and when they do 'tis the Devil's own chants they rend.'

Though he was only eight when the plague first swept through Hambledon, he would frequently regale anyone who cared to listen (and not many did nowadays), 'That were real death, not like th' plague of the sixties which, thanks to God, just touched upon us. This were real death, knocked down the strongest man and choked th' life out of 'im in three days—less sometimes.'

He had watched Mr. David Bonn, the vicar, buried less than four months after his arrival in Hambledon, and three uncles and many kinsmen. God had spared him, his father and mother. He also remembered the extra hours which those who survived—even children—worked in the fields helping the families who had lost their menfolk to gather in their harvests, without which they would surely starve.

With the back of his calloused, arthritic hand he wiped away the moisture which had gathered round his rheumy eyes, and thought of the hard and bitter years following the Black Death. He and his like, who survived, soon realised that their labour was now worth considerably more than before, and all over the country, so he had heard, the villeins asked for unheard of rewards. Though certain laws were passed easing their lot, some less scrupulous landlords continued with a heavy and oppressive hand to maintain their land and their villeins under the old conditions. Their villeins escaped and offered their services to other landlords who were prepared to ask no questions and pay more than the new maximum allowed.

There resulted bitterness and oppression, a sort of underground civil war all over the country between masters and workers. Then came the 'Boons', a scurrilous law by which a landlord could require his villeins to work extra days without remuneration, particularly if rain was expected and he wanted his crops gathered in time. This often meant that the poor peasants' crops were beaten down by autumnal storms.

---

*Tom Plowman is an imaginary character, but his reminiscences and the named people in them, except Martha his wife, are drawn from fact.

'Dear Mary, Mother of God,' thought Tom, 'I don' feel meself today.' He settled back on his bench and allowed the sun to warm him. An old grey-muzzled sheepdog bitch belonging to the ale house appeared around a corner of the building and nuzzled his gnarled hand.

Tom's mind wandered along the years to 1379. He did not know then that once again the Royal Treasury yawned with emptiness due to inept government and the prolonged war with France, but he knew its effect—the Poll Tax. He was quite an old man of 39 then, and he and his three sons who had reached the age of 15 had had to pay the three 'thickpennies' now demanded. That year the crops failed. His wife died and so did his youngest son, then scarcely one year old. He reflected bitterly that they might have lived, or at least had a better chance of recovery, if there had been sufficient bread to eat.

The Poll Tax, on top of the penny his family paid on every hearth and the tithes, was an impossible burden. But the lord of the manor's steward at the manor house was a fair man and had done much to relieve the misery of his people.

'Not,' thought Tom, 'like the last vicar, Mr. William de Clere. But 'e got 'is just deserts. In '76 it were when 'e was strangled in 'is bed. Though 'twere wrong,' mused the old man, 'for them what did it to have made off with 'is belongings.'

A faint smile creased Tom's lined and worn face. The bishop had never found out who had killed his vicar, but he knew, and all the pressure of the thumbscrews, all the torture of the rack would never have dragged it out of him. He remembered the bishop's brief, which had been read out in church afterwards:

> Certain satellites of Satan, sons of perdition, sunk in the depths of evil, whose names moreover and persons are unknown, lately entered the house of the vicarage of the church of Hambledon of our diocese clandestinely and at night, breaking and tearing asunder door and locks, attacked Mr. William, the last vicar there, priest, as he lay in his bed, inflicted wounds upon him, feloniously strangled and slew him, and not content with these things, they carried off secretly and nefariously from the said vicarage some goods which belonged to the said vicar.

''Twere brave,' mused Tom, 'but 'twere wrong to steal.'

The old man's thoughts returned to 1379. Great things began that year. At first whisperings reached the village, and later strange, terrifying ideas began to spread throughout the country. The peasant's priest, John Ball, who was preaching openly an end to villeinage, was advocating that peasants should rent their holdings at four pence an acre. There was also an open outcry against the accursed boons. John Ball's famous saying, 'When Adam delved and Eve span—who was then the gentleman?', reached and found receptive ears in every village in the country. But Tom remembered also the uncertainty, especially among the older members of the community, and the dread of reprisals.

During the following year this uncertainty vanished. A great undercurrent of resentment surged anew as a result of the second Poll Tax, which was even more unjustly graded than the first. It was then that all the villages around Hambledon, all the villages in the land, knew that rebellion must come. Then came the summer when the story spread that a tiler's daughter in Kent had been assaulted and ravished by a Poll

Tax collector. This was a gross exaggeration and the true facts were later told and retold around the villages of England. This tax collector, a hated man of a hated class, had accused a Kent tiler by the name of Wat of disguising his son as a daughter, and had torn the kirtle off her shoulders to prove his point. In fact he was mistaken, but this single act so incensed Wat Tyler that he dashed the groat-collector's brains out with his hammer.

In the early days of June 1381 Tom knew a rebellion was imminent; the atmosphere was tense, peasants tight lipped went about their work, waiting—waiting—for what they scarcely knew, but ready for anything that might be required of them. At last outright violence broke out. Kent and the south-eastern counties were the scenes of most of the active rebellion under various leaders, including Wat Tyler, but the spirit spread like a forest fire. In some villages manor houses were sacked, and elsewhere records defining services due from the villeins were burned. But this did not occur in Hambledon, for the lord of the manor had been fair according to the custom of the times, and the peasants respected this, but they were ready for any unified action required of them.

The old man recalled the day the great news arrived in Hambledon that the embattled tillers of the soil had taken over the city of London. The demand for an end to villeinage must now surely be met. Soon all men would rent their own holdings.

The whole strange rising only lasted a fortnight, but even though the villeins of Kent and the south-eastern counties controlled London for a short time it was ultimately a failure—as it was bound to be. The leaders, Tom admitted to himself, wouldn't have known how to use victory—no more than he would. Yet now all his grandchildren were free men; they and their children would always be so.

Tom shut his aching eyes. The old dog returned and nuzzled his hand again for more attention. He caressed her for a while until she walked off and lay down heavily in the dusty roadway. Tom, alone once more with his thoughts, recalled the day he first returned home drunk with ale. His mother had lashed him with her tongue, but his father had laughed and, giving him a friendly cuff over the head which had set his ears ringing and sent him sprawling across the earth floor, had bellowed, 'Chip off 'e old block!'

Suddenly his nostrils caught the smell of new-mown hay, which introduced a new train of thought. He saw a lithe, dark, wisp of a girl smiling at him through the years. 'My girl—my girl, Martha.'

He recalled the months he had spent wooing her in the late fifties, and the summer evening shortly before they were married when they had made their way to the hay meadows, where beneath the friendly cover of the gathering darkness and amid the smell of new-mown hay she had first become his. A smile creased the old man's face as his head sank on his chest.

The old sheepdog bitch seemed to sense that something had changed. She approached and sniffed the calloused hand and found it still and unresponsive. Her tail drooped and she backed away whining.

Cottage at Cams on Hill.

Chapter Six

The Market Town

The years between 1400, when Richard II died mysteriously in Pontefract Castle, and 1485, when Richard III fell at Bosworth Field, were coloured by futile and destructive wars—rebellions at home, the prolonged and finally disastrous war with France and then the cruel, ruthlessly fought faction fights at home, culminating in the Wars of the Roses. They were not happy years. On top of all this strife the people of England had to endure pestilence and famine, brigandage inland and piracy along the coasts.

There was one break in this inglorious period. In 1413 the dark clouds of misery which had been settling over England were flung back by the dazzling brilliance of Henry V. But only nine short years after his accession to the throne, during his great campaign in France, this athletic and powerful man was struck down by a mysterious illness which left the royal physicians at a loss. He walked with a laboured step and occasionally stumbled under the weight of his armour. In the early hours of 31 August 1422 he asked his physicians, 'How long have I to live?' With great reluctance they replied, 'Sire, not more than two hours.'

This time they were right.

After his death dark clouds settled once more over England, to remain during all the long years of the reigns which were to follow.

By mid century lawlessness abounded. The Channel was infested with pirates who sacked and plundered towns on the coast, and the Burgundian fleet began to harry the eastern and southern seaboards of England. It is possible that a number of Hambledon men left the village to take up arms against these raiders. In 1487 there was a commission to John Goldsmith* and others, appointing them to

> array and try all men at arms, and other fencible men, as well as hobelers** and archers, within the hundreds of Meonstoke, Hambledon and Waltham, County of Southampton, to lead them to the sea coast, and other places in the County, to resist

---

* 14 generations back from the author   ** Light horsemen

the King's enemies and to take the muster of the same from time to time, and cause watches to be kept, and bekyns to be set up in the usual places.

In 1485, when the conflict between the White Rose of York and the Red Rose of Lancaster was brought to a bloody close on Bosworth Field, there were probably not more than three million unhappy, weary people in England. For the minute fraction of this number who lived in Hambledon, life went on much as before. Men went off to the wars, work went on in the fields and more additions were made to the church.

A new main south doorway was built with a handsome porch of two storeys around it, and a two-storeyed chamber was added to the south-west corner of the church, which is now the vestry. The upper floors were removed, probably during the Victorian restoration, but the internal doorways, which opened onto a gallery connecting the two upper rooms, remain, and one of the old doors can still be seen high up in the south wall. In 1990 the upper floor above the vestry was restored with access from the vestry itself and it now serves as a very pleasant upper room for Sunday schools, meetings or small social events. The pulpit is also 15th-century as are the two Perpendicular windows in both the north and south aisles. (The window near the north-west angle of the nave was inserted in 1876 in imitation of the 15th-century windows which it was intended to match.) The roofs of the eastern nave and aisles are thought to be older than this century but the moulded timbers of the western nave are of this period.

16 Interior view of Hambledon church. The congregation begins to arrive for Easter Communion, 1994. Two hundred and fifty people were present, with ages ranging from seven months to 91 years.

During the Easter or Christmas seasons the mummers might have visited the village. Their allegorical plays, which have their origins in the 12th century predating the miracle and mystery plays, represented the struggle between the powers of good and evil for the possession of a human soul. Standard characters would include a king, a doctor, a Turkish knight and Beelzebub. The dialogue, reproduced here with modern spelling for ease of comprehension, would possibly contain the following:

King: Oh is there even a noble doctor to be found
          To cure this English Champion
          Of his deep and deadly wound?

Doctor: Oh yes there is a noble doctor to be found
          To cure this English Champion
          Of his deep and deadly wound.

King: What can you cure?

Doctor: All sorts of diseases
          Whatever you pleases,
          I can cure the itch, the pitch,
          The pthinc, the palsey and the gout.
          If the devil's in a man
          I can fetch him out.

King: What is your fee?

Doctor: Ten pounds is true.

King: Proceed noble doctor
          You shall have your due.

Enter Beelzebub ...

One can imagine the widened eyes and all but hear the gasps.

The following century, the century of Henry VIII, Mary Tudor and Elizabeth I, was remarkable to Hambledon only for the religious conflicts which touched city, town and village. In England, as in every other European country, the church had become worldly and corrupt; great resentment grew against the Popes and the wealth and luxury of the greater clergy. In 1534 the complex manoeuvres between England and Rome came to an end; the breach was final and King Henry VIII became head of the Church in England. For a while the change remained purely political, and Hambledonians saw no differences in the doctrine or in the ritual of the services in their church.

Four years after the break with Rome, the government ordered from Paris a large-scale printing of bibles in English. This was, in part, a measure against those who still objected to the Reformation and the suppression of the monasteries. In September 1583 every parish in the country was compelled by law to purchase one and install it in their church. Thus, in this year, Hambledon acquired its first bible in the English language. Undoubtedly it was at once avidly read by those who could read. It is not difficult to imagine the groups of peasants who would gather in the church on weekday evenings as well as on church festivals and Sundays to hear someone read aloud from the new bible.

However, it was not long before the conflict between Catholic and Protestant became bitter, even fanatical under Catholic Mary. Later, in the 1560s during Protestant Elizabeth's calmer approach to the problem, an attempt was made to persuade the mass of Catholics to accept the new order by the introduction of a system of fines, growing gradually more severe, for non-attendance at church. Strict Catholics thus paid no worse penalty than a fine so long as they were not active in opposition. The majority went to church rather than pay, and soon became accustomed to the new service book. However, in Hambledon a comparatively large number (quoted as 16) paid fines rather than accept the new order of services.

In nearby Exton, though, things did not turn out so happily for a second John Goldsmith to raise the ire of the Church. He had married Susan Tichbourne and in 1580 Bishop Watson had him committed to the common gaol because his wife was 'Obstinate in her Poperie and would not come to church, whilst he refused to enter into bonds for her conformity.' John Goldsmith however was sufficiently influential to have the ear of the Royal Council, with the result that in February 1581 the bishop was ordered to release him for the following rather quaintly expressed reasons: 'Their Lordships are credibly given to understand that the said Goldsmith is not able to overrule his wife's pevish disposicion in that behalf ... he, that is the Bishop, is required to give order presently for his enlargement and that the correction for her obstancie be layed upon her own carcas in case she shall contynie willful disposicion in refusing to come to church.'

Regardless of religious conflict, fishing, hunting and game rights remained as jealously guarded as ever by lords of manors. One Sunday in 1535, young Peter Norton, of whose family we shall hear more in the next century, called at the house of Sir Anthony Windsor in East Meon. He asked if he might borrow one of Sir Anthony's servants to accompany him to Hambledon. Leave being given, the two men set off, but, instead of keeping to the highway, they went straight to the Forest of Bere where Lord Lisle had overall responsibility for the safekeeping of the king's herds. There Peter Norton's greyhounds came across a buck and killed it. Returning to Sir Anthony's house with their prize, Peter Norton gave Sir Anthony half and took the other half home to his father, Sir Richard Norton. It was not long before Lord Lisle's keeper and his hounds tracked the miscreants back to the house in East Meon, and as a result Sir Anthony wrote a peculiarly grovelling letter to Lady Lisle: '... I know right well they will make a grievous matter to my lord of it ... Good Madam, though my servant and this young man hath done lewdly and have deserved punishment, I beseech you, Madam, to move my lord to be a good lord to them.' Sadly history does not relate how my lord was moved.

With the dawning of the 17th century the now prosperous manor of Hambledon stood poised and ready, amid the flow of years, for the second great date in its story—1612.

The illustrious Tudor dynasty ended with the death of good Queen Bess in 1603, and an unknown, alien king from Scotland, James I, succeeded to the Crown of England.

In the following year Thomas Bilson, Bishop of Winchester, was appointed to act as chief aid to Dr. Miles Smith, who was gathering about him the team of 47 men—theologians, scholars and professors of Greek and Hebrew—who were to undertake the task of writing the authorised version of the bible. Dr. Smith, born the son of a butcher in Hereford, was an orientalist who spoke Chaldaic, Syriac and Arabic, a 'stout and worthy scholar' who died Bishop of Gloucester. He was an extreme Protestant, and Bilson, a traditionalist, served to establish a balance between High Church and Puritanical views. The result of their labour, the much-loved King James Bible, with its noble and beautiful language, was published in 1611 and found from the very first a special place in the hearts of the people, which was to last for more than 300 years.

It was in the following year, 1612, that James I granted to Thomas Bilson, presumably in recognition of his work in the production of the new bible, the right to hold two fairs a year in Hambledon, in addition to the weekly market on Tuesdays. The first of these fairs was held on the second of February, the Feast of the Blessed Virgin Mary, 'in a field near Hambledon on the east', probably where the lovely Regency house called Fairfield now stands. The second fair was held on 21 September, the Feast of St Michael, 'in the town'. Letters patent for holding the fairs were stamped with the words 'Broad Halfpenny', which was the toll paid to the lord of the manor for setting up booths.

It was not long after 1612 that the 'cultivated lands of Hamelanduna' of 650 years before assumed the status of a market town. A large market hall existed, but little is known of this except that it fell down in 1819 during the years of Hambledon's decline. No one today knows for certain where it stood, but it was probably somewhere at the bottom of the High Street (or North Street as it was called in those days). A shop in this area is still called 'The People's Market'.

James I, the first king of 'Great Britain', died in 1624 and was succeeded by his son Charles I. Unperturbed, Hambledon flourished and thrived, grew in stature and prospered, unchecked by the civil war between King and Parliament which broke out in 1642. The loyalties of the manor were as divided as those of the country itself. There were in Hambledon some staunch supporters of the king, and of a particularly merry Cavalier we shall hear more later. However, the 'Hambledon Boys' fought on the Roundhead side under Colonel Richard Norton.

Sir Richard Norton of Southwick was a successful cavalry leader and an intimate friend of Cromwell, who wrote of him as 'idle Dick Norton'. His exploits during the war were legion, and it may be assumed that Hambledon men took part in most of them. The Rev. G. N. Goodwin in his book *The Civil War in Hampshire (1642-1645)* mentions them in his description of the Cheriton fight on 29 March 1644: 'Colonel Norton ... is said to have brought up his renowned troop of Hambledon Boys and charged the Cavaliers in the rear, thus not a little contributing to the victory.'

In 1645 the cause of King Charles I was desperate. Only a few outlying districts and castles held out for him, and their fall was certain. When, in the spring of 1646, the Parliamentary armies prepared to besiege Oxford, he slipped away from that city and surrendered himself to the Scots, and so ended the first phase of the war.

17 Fairfield House c.1905. From 1612 one of Hambledon's fairs was held 'in a field near Hambledon on the east'. Fairfield was probably built on that site.

18 Wounded from the First World War convalescing at Fairfield in 1916.

On 9 October Parliament issued an ordinance to give effect to the abolition of the Episcopacy. The estates of the bishops were placed in the hands of trustees, surveys of each manor were made and manors sold as purchasers were found. The manor of Hambledon was sold by Parliament in 1650 to George Wither, a poet and hymn writer for £3,796 18s. 11d. Wither's hymn book was probably the earliest of the post-reformation Church of England, and though it had momentary popularity it also aroused great opposition. A contemporary critic stated it was before its time; the production of such a book, though needed, could not be achieved by the work of one person. George Wither was an extraordinary man. He was brash and he was rash and his wilder writings frequently landed him in deep trouble, but he was a survivor, and despite his almost total lack of diplomatic skill he always seemed to emerge unscathed. He had been captured in the war and taken before the king at Oxford. He even escaped with his life on this occasion. It is said that a self-styled poet and Cavalier, Sir John Denham, pleaded successfully for his life on the grounds that while George Wither remained alive, he—Sir John—could not be accounted the worst versifier in the country.

The survey of Hambledon was made in 1647, a year after the abolition of the Episcopacy. It was carried out by a number of sworn jurors and it filled 20 closely written pages, which are now in the possession of the Ecclesiastical Commissioners.

They recorded three 'Demesnes', namely 'Hamuldon ffarme' (the Manor Farm), 'Teggles' (Teglease) and The Park. The arable lands of Hambledon Farm amounted to 275 acres (much the same as the acreage recorded in the 1320 survey which had so infuriated Alexander, Prior of Winchester) but now (1647) 'Teggles ... with all that Sheepp Walke adjoining', another 275 acres, had been added. The two farms were now 'both comprehended into Hamuldon ffarme with two manshon howses'.

They recorded the value of the manor (which was the annual income from the village enjoyed by the lord of the manor) as £68 2s. 10d. (In 1340 the value of Hambledon was assessed for tax purposes as £14 13s. 4d.)

Several stretches of common land and many of the rights and customs pertaining to them are mentioned. There was Hambledon Chase, whose 1,200 acres swept round the south of the manor from Catherington to Ervills, also Chidden Holt, West Chidden Downs, the East Chidden Downs and Broadhalfpenny. The lord of the manor had the hunting rights of the Chase which he guarded jealously, keeping a gamekeeper there, but he had no right of pasture for his cattle or sheep on any of the common lands. This was strictly the right, by custom, of the freehold and copyhold tenants of the manor, who were also allowed to cut underwood for fencing their grounds and had the right of first refusal of any trees felled before they were sold outside the manor. Chidden Holt and the East Chidden Downs were reserved only for the tenants of East Chidden, and no special rights were mentioned concerning Broadhalfpenny and the West Chidden Downs.

The copyhold tenants of the manor, of which there were about fifty-five, mostly paid money rents for their holdings, though a few paid in bushels or pecks of wheat and some paid in cocks and hens. Many of them paid 'harvist days' to the demesne farm. A copyholder was a man whose right to his land could only be shown in the copy of the rolls originally made by the steward of the lord of the manor's court. A freeholder held his property free of duty except to the king; there were 30 in Hambledon ranging from William Littlefield, with a house and garden, paying four pence a year, to the larger holders such as Sir Anthony Brewing and Sir Richard Norton, whose lands were described as manors within the manor. A few freeholders, however, appeared to owe 'plowdays' to the demesne farm.

Denmead, Ervills and part of Butvillians (modern Bittles) were described as other manors and small lordships within the manor of Hambledon. The other part of Butvillians had been owned by Winchester College since 1414.

The jurors also recorded that the lord of the manor held a Court Leet twice a year at the Feast of St Michael and at Easter, as had been the custom since the days of Magna Carta. A Court Baron, descendant of the old Hundred Court, was held every three weeks, and in addition a special court was held twice a year at which the tenants chose their reeve and beadle and other officers for service in the manor.

The vicarage at this time was in the hands of Mr. Charles Dean, who now paid two shillings a year for the benefice, from which he derived about £60 a year on which to live.

Comparing this survey with that which was carried out in 1320, we can see that in the intervening 300 years the serf had given way to freehold and copyhold tenants, of which there were about eighty-five; 587 more acres had been added to the arable lands of the demesne farm and in addition to the weekly market two fairs were now held every year. Furthermore, the centre of the Hambledon Hundred was now being called 'the town'. Nevertheless, life may be considered as having moved at a leisurely pace between 1320 and 1647, when one thinks of the 'progress' made in the next 300 years, which those who knew Hambledon in 1947 may judge for themselves.

By 1648 Lords and Commons, the great majority of townsmen and countrymen, the Scottish army and the English fleet—both of which had now changed sides—all turned against the hated New Model Army with Cromwell at its head. But their efforts were uncoordinated, and they lacked the uniform discipline of the Puritan Ironsides, who proved invincible. In 1648 the final rally to the Royalist cause ended in disaster when the Scottish army was destroyed at Preston. This rising led inevitably to the execution of Charles I. He was a man of many faults, but his end cut harshly across all that the English people held sacred—principle, tradition and custom. His death did not bring monarchy to an end, as Cromwell and his Puritans had hoped, but sanctified it.

***

Two soldiers entered the only ale house in Hambledon that now remained open, and William Plowman and his friends left. In silence they returned to their homes. Before the entry of the hated soldiers there had been some sporadic talk of the good old days under Charles I, but the atmosphere had been far from merry. Good days there had been, seen now in retrospect, and good days there would be again; but for the moment, in the 1650s, puritanical grimness had settled over Hambledon as it had over the whole country, city and village alike.

The parish register entries, hitherto meticulously penned, were now recorded in a random and illiterate manner either by the clerk or by the Presbyterian minister who

19 The High Street, *c*.1904. Note the *Red Lion Inn* on the right, one of Hambledon's eight public houses at the time. The *Bricklayer's Arms*, the *Red Lion*, and the *Green Man* are now private houses; the *Bell Inn* was pulled down. The *Vine*, the *New Inn*, the *George* and the *Bat and Ball* remain.

20 The People's Market in 1930.

had thrust out the Prayer Book from the church and the vicar from the vicarage. During the 11 years of the Commonwealth the Sacraments were abolished; there were no baptisms, children were registered as 'borne' on such and such a day and marriages became civil contracts. An example reads, 'A contract of Matrimonie between Anthony F. Foster and Mary Colfick was published on 27 of Sep and 4 of Oct and 11 Oct on the Lord's Daye and were married the 5th November 1657'.

Adultery had become punishable by death, all betting and gambling were forbidden, many ale houses had been closed and drunkenness carried hazards additional to the inevitable morning after. Swearing became punishable by a fine. A squire could be fined 10s. for his first offence, and it could cost the common people 3s. 4d. to relieve their feelings—even then they were not allowed much for their money. Such mild expressions as 'S'trewth' (God's truth) or 'Upon my life!' could cost the authors according to their station.

Religious feastdays, which had for so long proved such a welcome break from toil in the fields, were now considered as superstitious indulgences, and were replaced by a monthly day of fasting. Parliament in far away London was deeply concerned at the opportunities Christmas gave for carnal and sensual delights; as a result bewildered families in Hambledon and throughout the country had to suffer a Christmas season pruned of everything that could lead to happiness. Bemused at first, then bitter and angry, men longed for the time when the King would enjoy his own again.

In Hambledon, as in other villages, diversions which had before brought some joy into the lives of the villagers—bear baiting, cockfighting, athletic sports, horse racing and wrestling—were now all banned. It was not even permissible to take a Sunday walk; furthermore, in Hambledon the maypole had just been cut down lest the traditional dances that took place around it should lead to levity and immorality.

Never had any ruler been so hated as Cromwell, his Major Generals and all his minions. 'God rot the whole pox'd whore's spawn,' mouthed William Plowman as he kicked open the door of his house, and his friends hurried away.

Chapter Seven

Royal Roundhead

The news of King Charles I's execution on 30 January 1649 was not long in reaching Hambledon. Some there were in the manor who suddenly felt that all their troubles were at an end, though many, like William Plowman, were soon to change their minds as Puritan grimness settled over the village. Others were profoundly shocked, but they had to be careful what they said in public, for they were now living in what today we would call a police state.

Thomas Symons of Hambledon was such a man. He was a bluff, hail-fellow-well-met yeoman farmer who lived to the south of the village in the house that was later to be called Bury Lodge. The house was pulled down in 1800. Twenty-five years ago, in the 1970s, the vague outlines of the cellar, that Symons had always kept so well stocked, could be seen. Today they are completely obscured by creeping ivy, tree roots, leaf mould and the criss-cross tracks of foxes, deer and badgers. Symons had done well for himself, and expansive middle-age suited him. Before the troubles began he was widely admired and respected, especially by those who enjoyed a joke with their ale. He was, in his own way, a devout man and a regular churchgoer, but there were many now who regarded him with deep suspicion; his open-handed ways, his loud voice, his levity and his coarse jests were the hallmark of the ungodly, of Satan himself. Also— and Thomas Symons never spoke seriously on this subject in public—he was a staunch supporter of the Cavalier Cause, and his wife, Ursula, was the sister of a Cavalier Colonel, George Gounter.

His hopes, and the hopes of those like him, had risen when it became known that the exiled Prince of Wales had been recognised by the Scots as King Charles II and that he had landed in Scotland. Then followed a time of uncertainty during which rumours became harder to distinguish from truth. The news that the Scots were planning to invade England with King Charles released another flood of rumours concerning the conditions they intended to impose should they win.

In 1650 Cromwell marched his invincible Ironsides into Scotland, and in September of that year news reached Hambledon of his spectacular victory at Dunbar. This was

21 Bury Lodge, 1994. In 1800 Thomas Symons's house was pulled down and the new Bury Lodge was built further back from the road near the (then undiscovered) site of a Roman villa house.

followed by the news of the fall of Perth and then reports spread south that the Scots, under General Leslie, were marching towards London with the 21-year-old king.

These rumours hardened into fact as Cromwell pursued the invaders and met them at Worcester on 3 September 1651. There the English army annihilated the Scots and, although at one time it was thought that the king had been killed on the battlefield, the strongest rumours suggested that Charles II had escaped with a small party of loyal supporters. A proclamation posted in Hambledon towards the end of September, to the effect that a reward of £1,000 would be paid to anyone coming forward with information that would lead to the arrest of Charles Stuart, seemed to confirm these stories.

Sunday, 12 October 1651, was a depressing day. In Hambledon it rained from early morning until night; the unbroken layers of black cloud reflected exactly the dark mood of Mr. Thomas Symons. In the morning he went to church from which he returned home full of choler and bile, and was several times very rude to his wife. Occasionally he would look out at the rain, curtains of water moving up the valley from the south-west, and over and over again he would ponder the question—'Where would be an end to all these troubles?'

On the same Sunday in October 1651, Colonel Robin Phelips, tired, dirty and very wet, rode into Heale, a small village a few miles from Salisbury. Phelips was a sombre Cavalier of enormous physical strength and endurance. His heavy, craggy face seldom wore a smile, his general expression was one of dull, stolid severity. No one could describe him as intelligent, for he was so lacking in this quality that he was guided almost entirely by instinct. However, his lack of intelligence was offset by his stupendous loyalty to his master, the fugitive king, whom he worshipped and guarded as a great watchdog might.

King Charles at this time was hiding at Heale House, anxious and tired, his hair cut short and wearing mean, drab clothes not likely to attract unwanted attention. The purpose of Colonel Phelips' journey was to report to the king that his colleague, Colonel George Gounter, had, after a difficult search, found a sea captain at Brighthelmstone (Brighton) who was prepared to carry him to France. He was then to conduct the king along a prearranged route through Warnford to Hinton Daubnay, the house of Mr. Lawrence Hyde, two miles east of Hambledon, where they were to spend the night.

Colonel Gounter, in his search for a loyal and trustworthy captain who would convey 'a small party of distressed Cavaliers' to France and be discreet about it, had had no more than eight hours snatched sleep in the last four days. Throughout that same wet Sunday he slept soundly till dusk in the house of Mr. Anthony Brown, also near Hambledon. Under the same roof, Lord Wilmot, who had been with the king since Worcester, fussed and fretted, restlessly pacing the rooms, not daring to go outside. After Gounter awoke he and Lord Wilmot discussed alternative plans, for neither was happy about the king staying Monday night at Hinton Daubnay as it was too well known as a Royalist household. Gounter undertook to find an alternative, and suggested that they spend the Monday morning on the downs if the weather allowed.

The weather did allow. On Monday the sun rose over Hambledon in cloudless splendour. Thomas Symons felt much better. He had a good breakfast, joked around the house and was especially pleasant to his wife. At about 10 o'clock he called for his horse and, having made a tour of his small demesne, he set off for a neighbouring village where he was due to lunch with a friend. After his departure, Ursula Symons set about the numerous duties that kept a yeoman housewife busy. Later in the morning a servant came and told her that the Colonel had called and wished to see her. Not knowing quite which Colonel to expect she went into the hall. To her astonishment and delight, standing in the sunlit porch was her brother, George Gounter, immaculate as usual but not so obviously the Cavalier as in days gone by.

'It does me good to see you again, my dear Ursula,' said the Colonel as he followed his sister into the house. 'It's been a weary while since we met. But I may not remain at this time, for I have come to borrow a brace of greyhounds, if Thomas can spare them. Our cousin Tom Gounter and other gentlemen are upon the downs and have a mind to course at a hare.'

'Of course you may have them, but 'tis ill favour that you come not near me for a year and then only to borrow Tom's dogs!'

'I feared you'd say as much,' replied the colonel, putting his arm round his sister's waist, 'but I'm promised. Tell me, Ursula, are you expecting company this evening?'

Ursula Symonds shook her head.

'Then, what say you, if we beat not too far with Tom's good hounds, that we all of us come and make merry with you and Tom tonight?'

'You will be most heartily welcome. You may be sure of a good supper and comfortable beds afterwards—but, George, how many will there be?'

Gounter counted the party off on his fingers: 'There'll be Tom Gounter and ....,' the colonel had a quick mental vision of the portly and noble-looking Lord Wilmot, who had used a number of names in the last few weeks, '... a Mr. Barlow of Devonshire, also a Colonel Phelips and the son of a poor yeoman tenant of Barlow's Devon estate named William Jackson and Barlow's servant Swan and myself, 'tis six all told.'

At that moment a man brought round the two greyhounds and George Gounter took his leave. He declined a tankard of ale but called over his shoulder as he rode away, 'Tell Tom he may be sure of his dogs.'

On the sun-drenched downs around Hambledon he met Lord Wilmot and his cousin Tom, and for a time they beat about the downs for hare, but without success. Their hearts were not in their sport, for the recurrent anxiety concerning the plan to get King Charles to France (which had miscarried three times) was uppermost in their minds. For nearly six weeks such plans had been made and had failed, and the narrowness of some of the monarch's escapes was nerve-shattering. Everything now depended on Robin Phelips who was enduring his third day in the saddle. So much could go wrong, for the loyal old soldier was capable of the most extraordinarily foolish actions.

Finally all appetite for coursing left the worried Cavaliers. It was decided that Lord Wilmot and Tom Gounter should ride back to Hambledon, return Symons' greyhounds and later rendezvous with the royal party on the downs to the north of Hambledon. Colonel George Gounter made his way towards Warnford. He rode around Hambledon towards Broadhalfpenny Down and from there cut across, north of Chidden, to Old Winchester Hill, past the Iron Age fort and down to Warnford. By the time he was approaching Warnford it was well into the afternoon and doubts began to assail him. Had he missed the king? Had Colonel Phelips lost his way? Worse still, had they fallen among enemies? He decided to ride on for another hour and then, if he had not met with the king, to return direct to Mr. Lawrence Hyde's house, Hinton Daubnay, where arrangements had been made for the king to spend the night.

Gounter had just entered the outskirts of Warnford when he first saw them. Phelips was wearily riding ahead, very much the Cavalier gentleman, dressed in almost complete disregard for the new trend towards simple attire, and behind him, hair shorn and in a dusty, dull grey suit devoid of all lace, was the king. Gounter learned later that Colonel Phelips had not at all like the idea of preceding his monarch, but the king had insisted on playing the role of the colonel's poor travelling companion to the full. (He had already been a serving man, a groom and a runaway bridegroom of poor estate.)

As there were people about and they were among houses, Gounter pretended not to know the two travellers coming from the opposite direction, and rode past them making no sign of recognition. At the first inn he came to he stopped, and having purchased some tobacco, he drank a glass of ale with relish and then retraced his steps at a smarter pace, overtaking the king and Colonel Phelips near Old Winchester Hill. George Gounter had not as yet met the king, for his part in the plan had been to find a sea captain that could be trusted and to make the arrangements for the king's sailing to France.

He was therefore rather startled when a merry voice shouted out, 'Is this my new guardian who deigns not to recognise so mean a party in the public street? I'm very glad to see you, Colonel Gounter!'

George Gounter snatched off his hat and, pressing his horse close to the king's, took his hand and kissed it.

'Your Majesty! God be praised ... '

'None of your "Majesties" now,' reproved the king, pulling a heavy frown in mock severity over his ugly young face. 'You are the first in rank like good Robin Phelips here; I take second place. Where is my Lord Wilmot?'

'Sire, if you will ride on to the down above Hambledon, about two miles hence, my lord awaits us there.'

From Old Winchester Hill they rode on in company until they reached Broadhalfpenny Down, where, at that spot of land that was to achieve immortality in the next century, they met Lord Wilmot, Tom Gounter and Wilmot's servant, Swan. The party paused. The king asked Wilmot about Mr. Hyde and Hinton Daubnay; Lord Wilmot and Colonel Phelips spoke together. 'I like it not ...' began Wilmot, but Colonel Phelips' booming voice drowned the rest of my lord's reply. 'He has a fine house, Hinton Daubnay, a fine house worthy of the occasion.'

Charles demurred about the house, and fearing an unwise or extravagant reception awaiting him, he declared he would rather stay at a smaller place.

Turning to Lord Wilmot he asked, 'What say you, Harry?'

'I like it not,' repeated Wilmot. 'It is altogether too large and too well-known as Royalist for safety. And besides I have stayed there overmuch myself during the past week.'

The king looked questioningly at Colonel Gounter, who immediately thought of Symons' house in Hambledon—small, unpretentious and safe. It was no accident that that very morning he had lightly suggested to his sister that she might have company that night.

'Sire, my sister lives in Hambledon down yonder,' he said, indicating the way to the village, 'and I happen to know that the house is free this evening with but my sister and her husband, one Thomas Symons.'

'And how about Master Symons?' asked the king.

'Thomas Symons is a loyal and trustworthy fellow, merry to a fault but dependable; also of course, he need not be told of your ...' he was about to say 'Majesty's' '... your true identity.'

The king made up his mind. 'Some gaiety would do us well. We will call upon the hospitality of your kind sister and her good husband. Do you ride ahead and warn her of our coming, Colonel Gounter.'

'There is no need, sire. I took the liberty this very morning of telling my sister that a party of gentlemen might call upon her this evening. If my lord will be content to remain Mr. Barlow of Devonshire and you, sire,—if you would remain, as I have been instructed by my lord ...'

'Will Jackson. Aye, it pleases me well,' interrupted the king. 'Come, let us on our way.'

Wishing to avoid the village, they skirted Glidden and Rushmere as dusk began to gather in the valley of Hambledon below them. They then followed the track from Rushmere down to Symons' house, and 'at candle-lighting' they stood before his door.

Thomas Symons had had a very good day. Work was going well round his estate and he had lunched prodigiously with his friend, after which they had spent the remainder of the afternoon together drinking, talking and 'setting the world to rights again'. Thomas was late returning to Hambledon, and, as he had to pass one of the village inns on the way to his house, he stopped there. The ale he had taken with his friend had passed its natural course, and he now felt the urge for more ale and more congenial company. He found both. It was quite dark when he got home, where he was delighted to learn from his servant that 'the Colonel' and other guests had arrived.

Pushing his way past his man, he flung open the door of the parlour with a dramatic welcome on his tongue, but the room was quite empty.

'God's teeth,' he muttered, as the noise of company came to him from the dining parlour. With only slightly less bombast he threw open the door to this room and found his wife and guests halfway through their supper. He greeted his wife, who had risen to meet him, with a playful bussing and warmly greeted his brother-in-law, then with-out waiting for introductions, declared in a slightly thickened voice, 'God's teeth! Is this what happens when a man's out of his house an hour or so? But 'tis brave to see such noble company. You're welcome! You're welcome!'

He was about to address the noble-looking Lord Wilmot when he caught sight of King Charles and froze. The king, warmed by the peace and security this house had hitherto offered, was relaxed and had forgotten his role of Mr. Barlow's poor tenant's son. Thomas Symons instantly mistrusted this man, whom he did not recognise, and turned to his brother-in-law.

''S teeth, man, who is this? I declare you have dishonoured me by bringing a scurvy Roundhead under my roof.'

There was a stunned silence. Ursula Symons said sharply, 'Thomas!'

Colonel Phelips was outraged and rose grandly to his feet, only to be pulled back by George Gounter and silenced with a look from King Charles. Lord Wilmot was for once at a loss for words.

'He is no Roundhead,' said Gounter. 'He's a staunch and true friend ...'

'No Roundhead?' shouted Symons, swaying slightly from heel to ball of toe. 'Look at him! Now here,' indicating the assembled company in general and the acutely embarrassed Colonel Phelips in particular, 'we have a gentleman and a gallant soldier to boot and so, my dear brother-in-law, do we have in you—and in young Tom Gounter over there. But if he is no Roundhead, mark upon it he's a spy.'

'Thomas, be still.' George Gounter's voice now carried command. 'To this man whom you have so roundly abused under your own roof, I owe my life.'

Symons was mortified. He made his way over to where the king was sitting, clapped him over the shoulder, sat down beside him and said, ''Tis a poxy coil i' faith! Forgive my rudeness, Brother Roundhead. All I have ...,' and here he suppressed the gathering pressure of a belch, '... is yours,' and with a blind grand-gesture he sent a glass of ale flying into Robin Phelips' lap.

Lord Wilmot sighed despairingly, for he had caught the gleam of merriment in the king's eye, and knew only too well that the chances of his bearing himself discreetly were remote. He also noticed that Colonel Phelips had turned an alarming crimson and was about to burst into indignant protests; he frowned at the colonel, who muttered something inaudible and bent over his plate.

'Brother, I thank you!' said the king, his eyes twinkling. 'I see you are an honest man.'

'An honest man? By God's breath, Brother Roundhead, so honest that the sight of a cropped head fair gives me an itch in the ...,' he caught his wife's eye, '... affects me like sour ale. Ale! A pox upon me! You have an empty glass. God's truth, all the glasses are full of air! Some ale! Some ale!'

Symons staggered to his feet and shortly returned with beer. When all the glasses were filled he stood before his guests and, looking directly at the king, he blurted out, 'I give you a toast—a damned good toast—to all damned, good and godly Roundheads.'

'That's too much!' snorted Phelips, and the king kicked his ankle under the table.

'I'll have no such toasts in my house,' said Mrs. Symons in a horrified voice, 'and as for you, Thomas Symons, you've drunk enough toasts for one night.'

Symons drained his glass and did not the see the king quickly exchange his full glass for the empty one Robin Phelips pushed towards him. Again the master of the house filled up all the glasses, while his wife said bitterly, 'I know not what devil is in him; he is not often thus.'

'My dear madam,' Lord Wilmot replied in his rich, cultured voice, 'a man who likes not his ale is no man for me.'

Symons, in refilling his own glass, had just poured a quantity of ale down his doublet, and an ear-splitting oath escaped his lips. Then, putting down his glass, he said more to himself than to anyone else, 'Oh dear brother, that was a 'scape. Swear not I beseech you, for we all be godly puritans here.'

Suddenly he threw himself into a burlesque of Roundhead behaviour—at least as he imagined it might be. Symons was a natural clown, and now, rather drunk, he was extraordinarily funny as he minced round the room, his head nodding like a hen in time with his step. Of all the laughter and ribald encouragement, the loudest came from the king, who was soon beyond words; head back, hands clutching his sides, he laughed fit to die. Even Robin Phelips, out of loyalty to his master, allowed his craggy face to break into a smile. The act was brought to a sudden close when Symons overreached himself and collapsed backwards onto a table, overturning a large bowl of flowers. He picked himself up. Then still in irrepressible humour, he returned to the table and replenished the empty glasses. Indeed, for the rest of the evening he plied his guests with strong waters and beer, paying particular attention to the king, whom he persisted in calling 'Brother Roundhead'. Charles was thoroughly enjoying himself for the first time in many days but, knowing he had an early start the next day, he did his utmost to avoid the never-ceasing flow of strong liquor. There was no convenient receptacle nearby, but when Symons was not looking he would pass his glass to either Phelips or Gounter, who would somehow get rid of the contents.

Before supper it had been decided that the two colonels, Mr. Barlow and Tom Gounter would sleep in the main house, but that owing to lack of space young 'William Jackson' would sleep in the adjoining cottage with Swan and the servants. Robin Phelips demurred at once, but the idea suited the king admirably and he conveyed his wishes to Colonel Gounter. And so at 10 o'clock Colonel Gounter conducted the king to bed. It was not long before the entire royal party, their merry host and his wife were all soundly asleep.

By the time the master of the house had managed to open his reluctant eyes to face the none too welcome light of Tuesday morning, King Charles, Lord Wilmot and Colonel Gounter were well on their way to Brighthelmstone. Colonel Phelips had made a bluff leavetaking on the downs above Hambledon. He had seized the king's hand, swept it to his lips and when he spoke his voice was thick with emotion.

'God be with you, Sire, and may it not be long ere you come to your throne.'

'Amen to that, Robin, and when I return be sure and let me see you.'

'I shall do so, sire.' The Colonel dropped the hand he was still gripping, turned his horse and left at a smart trot.

Tom Gounter and Wilmot's man, Swan, left the party at Stanstead. The shy Tom Gounter kissed hands briefly and rode home. Robert Swan also kissed the king's hand and made a short and very proper little speech of farewell, but when he turned to Lord Wilmot, with whom he had been since long before Worcester, emotion got the better of his voice.

'My lord,' he said, indicating the saddle trunk which had been transferred to Wilmot's horse, 'beneath your best linen are your handkerchiefs and between them I have laid your lordship's lace bands. Wrapped in a napkin and placed in the right corner are the roots for cleaning your lordship's teeth and the phial of musk.'

'I never thought you'd do it, Harry,' said the king as Swan drew out of earshot.

'I had to,' replied Wilmot seriously. 'I shall not be long without a servant, and he would not do in France.'

'But Harry, do not look to me to wait upon you because I will not do it.'

'My dear sir, I pray you leave off jesting.'

All that day they travelled east. In the evening they supped quietly at the *George Inn*, a small hostelry by the sea in a shabby fishing hamlet near Brighthelmstone; there they met Captain Tattersal. At about 2 o'clock on the Wednesday morning they set out for Southwick, another small village between Brighthelmstone and the mouth of the river Ardur. It was at Southwick that they first saw Captain Tattersal's barque, the *Surprise*. She was a small boat of not more than 60 tons and she lay heeled over, high and dry on the mud in the creek.

Having said their farewells to Gounter, the king and Lord Wilmot and Tattersal boarded the barque, while from a ruined hovel standing among the reeds and tamarisk

22 The Mazer presented by King Charles II to Hambledon's convivial Cavalier, Thomas Symons. It is now in the possession of the present owners of Bury Lodge, Major General and Mrs. Hew Butler.

23 King's Rest, 1994.

bushes along the foreshore the colonel watched the tide creeping in. By 8 o'clock the *Surprise* was off the mud. Slowly she drew away from the land, a dirty, dingy little barque carrying a king to safety.

Cold, exhausted, but with a deep sense of gratitude the colonel watched this sturdy little boat stand out to sea. The silence around him was broken only by the lapping of the waves on the muddy shore and the cries of the lonely gulls that wheeled above him against a dull grey sky. By midday the *Surprise* was just a speck on the skyline and ten minutes later she was out of sight beyond the grey horizon.

***

Two hundred and ninety-three years later, in very different circumstances, the king of England again visited Hambledon, where he reviewed his troops shortly before the Normandy landings in 1944. The parade took place in the Chestnut Meadow opposite Bury Lodge, which was then owned by Major General S. S. Butler. As the general was on leave at the time and the review was held on his land, it was natural that he should be invited to accompany the king throughout his short stay in Hambledon. So it was for a second time in the village's story that the owner of Bury Lodge acted as host to his king.

After the Restoration of Charles II (in 1660), Hambledon was returned to the Bishop of Winchester, with whom it remained until 1869, when it was taken over by the Ecclesiastical Commissioners. By the time King Charles had returned, George Gounter was dead, but the king adopted his son and educated him at Winchester and Oxford. To the convivial Symons he sent a superb *lignum vitae* mazer (a large, handsomely worked drinking vessel, primarily intended for punches). This mazer is now in the possession of Major General Hew Butler of Bury Lodge. The cottage where the king slept still stands and is known today as 'King's Rest'.

Houses at the top of High St where Mr Thurmwood had his School

Chapter Eight

Fire, Bells, Knells and Murder

The 18th century brought tragedy to Hambledon in the form of a disastrous fire and a particularly brutal murder. It also brought the manor to its most glorious moments on the cricket field at Broadhalfpenny Down.

Queen Anne ascended the throne in 1702, and for the five million people who populated England at this time, great days of power were soon to begin, as Britain laboured to bear her empire. In the world of letters it was the century of Addison, Swift, Defoe and Pope; it was also the century that saw Isaac Newton and Christopher Wren, Robert Walpole, the two Pitts, Clive and Warren Hastings, and the loss of the American colonies. It was the century in whose closing years there rose to early prominence a young admiral named Nelson, a young general called Arthur Wellesley and, in France, Napoleon Bonaparte.

In Hambledon, society fell broadly into three classes which merged so gradually into each other that there was no sharp distinction between them. (The great landowning magnates of England formed a fourth class which lived in splendour in princely mansions and virtually ruled the country. However no such family, of which there were about seventy in the kingdom, lived in the village.)

First in Hambledon came the 'squirearchy', men of substantial estates—manors and small lordships within the manor—who lived on their land and played a very active part in the affairs of the country. This class shaded imperceptibly into the 'yeomanry', some farming their own land and others renting farms. They formed a solid, prosperous middle class from which the higher classes were constantly recruited; as churchwardens and in positions of manorial responsibility they managed village business. Next came the vast majority, the 'peasantry', and here again there was no clear-cut distinction between the modest yeoman and the peasant who had done well for himself. They were not just wage-earning labourers, for many of them were smallholders in their own right, and even the day-labourers often supplemented their livelihood from their little holdings and their pasture rights on the common lands. In short, in the country areas of England, there existed a state of social harmony and contentment.

In 1714 George I arrived in England from Hanover. He was a singularly unattractive man who had locked up his wife for life and refused to speak to his son. He could not speak a word of English and made no effort to learn. Believing that the Tories aimed at removing him from the throne he was content to leave the conduct of affairs entirely in the hands of the Whigs.

In 1715 the miserable Jacobite conspiracies fizzled out. The rising in the south-west, which was aimed at involving the Tory gentlemen of the area, failed as did the planned rebellions in the north of England, Wales and the Highlands of Scotland. In Hambledon the following year, there occurred on Broadhalfpenny Down (where half a century later there was to be 'High Feasting' and great cricket) a strange riotous assembly led by the vicar, Mr. William Harby.

Affidavits sworn by Captain Benjamin Brady (of the late regiment of Brigadier Dalzele) and John Binsted and his son, both of Hambledon, paint a lurid picture of the events occurring on the afternoon of 4 April 1716, during horse races on Broadhalfpenny Down. The Binsteds with Captains Brady, Brown and Gibbon 'and several honest gentlemen in a peaceable manner were together in drinking the health of his Majesty King George, the Duke of Marlborough and several other Loyal healths when Mr. Harby, vicar of Hambledon, with several papists and other persons to the number of one hundred and more ... were assembled together at a Horse race to disturb the publick peace'. The Rev. Mr. Harby then assaulted young Binsted 'by pulling and wringing him by the Nose and soon after ... alighting from his horse (on which before he was) did come up to [John Binsted the younger] with a Stick or Club in his hand and did shake the same Stick at him ... and among other scurrilous expressions told [John Binsted] that he was an informing Dog, and that he would bury him before he went home'. John Binsted the elder complained that the said vicar 'did three times violently assault and beat [him] and that they did throw Sticks and Stones at him'. Captain Brady also confirms that sticks and stones were thrown, some of which 'strook' him. He confirmed on oath that a Mr. Caryll 'did at the same time reflect on the late Revolution and said that the Whiggs had breached into the Laws of the Nation'.

Unfortunately we do not have the reverend gentleman's side of the story. Suffice it to say he remained vicar of Hambledon for a further eight years until 1724.

Apart from high jinks on Broadhalfpenny Down the first quarter of the century passed peacefully. The cycle of life continued; crops were sown, tended, harvested and stored, men were born and reared, they died and were buried. In April 1724 Robert Taylor, a blacksmith living in East Street, made his last will and testament leaving all his possessions to his loving wife Alice. He must have died shortly after-wards, for by the last year in the reign of George I, when disaster struck the village, she was a widow.

It was one night in 1726 that the inhabitants of the houses in the High Street woke in terror to the dread cries of 'Fire!' An ugly pall of yellowish smoke was escaping through the upper windows and thatch of one of the houses on the east side of the street.

24   The High Street, *c.*1906. The great fire of 1726 probably started in one of the houses on the left (east) side of this street, most of which were destroyed. It is not known what occasion brought out all the boys and girls.

Thomas Bristow, who managed a business from his house near the corner, rushed out in horror and joined the men, women and children who were anxiously gathering outside. Some panicked, many rushed noisily to help, while others quietly did what they were told. Before the first chain of buckets from the nearest well could be organised the whole thatched roof suddenly exploded into flame. Several women screamed and the crowd drew back. Myriad sparks swirled into the air to be caught by a stiff westerly wind and blown down the line of Tudor houses and cottages lining East Street.

Above the crackle and roar of the flames, which now lit the entire High Street, the shouts of men mingled with the clanking of buckets and the hiss of combat as fire and water fought for mastery. The house in which the fire started suddenly collapsed in a roar of falling bricks, blazing timbers and spiralling sparks; almost at once two more houses burst into flames. The village manual pump had arrived by this time to add its pathetic squirt of water to the seemingly hopeless battle. Thomas Bristow was fortunate; the wind had borne the deadly sparks and burning fragments of thatch past his cottage. Some had lodged in the thatch of Fountain House in East Street. Its owner, John Mullens, and his family had fought to save what they could but, defeated by the intense heat, appalled and sickened, they could only watch as the flaming thatch collapsed onto the floor beneath it, and that floor collapsed onto the floor below that, until nothing but the blackened walls remained. His neighbour, Thomas Ewen, joined him with his family—exhausted by their efforts to save as many of their possessions as they were able. They, in turn, were joined by the weary and distressed Kennett family as their cottage collapsed with a thunderous roar and a great plume of flame surged upwards in a swirl of victory. By some extraordinary chance the home of John Courtnell, next door, was scarcely touched, but beyond it Alice Taylor's house, like so many others that night, was burned to the ground.

Many still fought the flames but, despite several human bucket-chains, the fire pump and the efforts of individuals trying to 'wet down' or save their property, the fire embraced house after house in its relentless sweep eastwards between Church Lane and East Street.

Every man and woman and many children too were finally engaged in what was now a desperate attempt to save the village. At times they seemed near to success, but always the accursed wind would carry the numberless sparks that rose when a house collapsed and would lodge them in the thatch of other houses. At about four in the morning the wind suddenly died, but the exhausted fire-fighters did not notice until the cry went up: 'The wind's dead!' Like a strength-giving elixir the news spread among the weary men and women who, with new-found energy, redoubled their efforts. Even the thin stream of water from the manual pump made its first inroads towards victory.

No one went back to bed that night. The sun rose over wide devastation, charred timbers, blackened bricks, burnt thatch, sodden half-burned beds, bedding, household goods and chattels. Wisps of smoke still rose here and there from the wreckage, and bands of men beat out smouldering material, while over the whole village hung the dank, unholy stench of fire. Knots of people were moving about the charred remains saving odd family possessions or perhaps looking for evidence of a missing child. Other groups were trying to comfort and help those who had lost their homes.

Most of the old houses on the east side of the High Street had been destroyed or badly damaged as were those on the north side of East Street. These latter were Tudor-built houses and cottages with jettied upper storeys. Some were burned to the ground, others like Fountain House were badly damaged with only walls left standing, and one or two, like the house of John Courtnell, were scarcely touched. The devastation was appalling.

Until recently we could only guess at the course of Hambledon's struggle that night. We did not even know (and still do not know) whether there was any loss of life due to this major fire which caused damage amounting to £5,184. Until the deeds of some of the houses in East Street came to light in the 1970s and '80s our only information about this disaster came to us through the briefs read in other parishes.

A brief was a letter of appeal sent out by the Lord Chancellor's office and read in churches after the Nicene creed. The Rubric of those days stated: 'Then shall the curate declare unto the people what Holy-Days or Fasting-Days are in the week following to be observed. And then also (if occasion be) shall notice be given of the Communion and Briefs, Citations and Excommunications read'.

The brief concerning the fire in Hambledon was read in many parishes throughout the country; collections were taken and solemnly recorded by churchwardens. Their precisely penned remarks were until very recently the only evidence we had of a night of terror in Hambledon:

25   East Street, *c.*1906. In 1726 there were no buildings on the site of the house on the extreme left, or where Mrs. Matthews shop stands. The house beyond, where John Courtnell lived, had a miraculous escape from the fire. The two houses beyond that were burned to the ground.

26   Further along East Street, *c.*1912. One of Hambledon's first cars approaching the smithy later owned by Fred Masey. The cottages on the left were pulled down in the 1950s.

BURGHCLERE, HANTS. 1726 collected by ye Briefe for Hambledon 2/3d.

SAXMUNDHAM. Collected here for a buring in Habledon in Coun South Hapton ye sum of three shillings and one penny April ye 27th, 1727.

LILFORD CHURCH, PETERBOROUGH. Hambledon in Coun Southampton; Loss by fire 5184 li. Collected November 13th 1726 - 0 0 10d.

NARBOROUGH, NORFOLK. 1726. 2nd October collected towards ye fire at Hambledon in ye county of Southampton - 5/8d.

NUTHURST, SUSSEX. Brief of 14/5/1727 re fire at Hambledon.

From the deeds of no.9 East Street we learn that in 1726 the blacksmith Robert Taylor's widow, Alice, was desperate. The house on which she held the residue of a 1,999-year lease was '... in the late dreadful conflagration at Hambledon burnt to the ground [and she] being in straightened circumstances was unable to rebuild'. Another indenture dated 1729 referring to the 1726 tragedy states: '... there happened a dreadful fire at Hambledon which burnt down the greatest part of the town ...'

(Alice's house was in fact rebuilt by her daughter's father-in-law, Thomas Outton, a wheelwright of West Dean, and she was allowed to live there for the rest of her life in exchange for the remainder of the lease.)

Fire was an ever-present threat where timber-framed, thatched cottages nestled together in picturesque proximity. Seventy-two years earlier, in midsummer 1654, there is a record of another major fire at Hambledon where nine dwelling houses were destroyed with loss in value of £777. Time and time again the Courts Leet and Baron in the Court House, East Street, declared and recorded, as in March 1757, that 'all persons living in the manor of Hambledon who suffer their chimneys to be dangerous to the damage of their neighbours, their fire flaming above the shaft shall forfeit for every offence three shillings and four pence'.

Above the High Street the old church looked down on occasions festive and tragic alike. In 1726 it witnessed the wreckage being cleared, the houses rebuilt in the contemporary Georgian style, and watched as the ugly wounds slowly healed.

At the time of the fire five bells in the church tower rang the peals that called the people to prayer, acclaimed a wedding or solemnly sounded the knell for some departed Hambledonian whose mortal remains had but one short journey to make. Then there came a day in 1749 when they were dismantled, lowered onto carts and began a long, slow journey to the foundry of Robert Catlin in London. The 13th-century tower became strangely silent.

For several years Hambledonians had been complaining of the poor quality of their church bells; it is possible also that the safety of the old tower was endangered when the biggest bell was in full swing. In any case it was decided to raise the money to have the five old bells recast into a peal of six. The vicar, John Sutton, and his churchwardens, John Horn and George Binsted, launched the appeal and, with the help of Captain S. Penfold and Mr. Thomas Charles, collected the necessary sum of money. Six new bells finally returned to Hambledon late that year or early in 1750 and were hung in the tower. Three of them have since had to be recast, one in 1882, one in 1918 and one in 1952, as may be seen from the inscriptions on the bells themselves which read as follows:

1. J. Taylor & Co. Founders, Loughborough 1882
   J.B. Barkworth paid for me.
2. Honi Soit Qui Mal e/y Pense. Junr. R.C.* 1749
3. Prosperity to all our benefactors.
   Robert Catlin cast us all 1749.
4. Robert Catlin, London Fecit 1749.
5. Mears and Stainbank London.
   The five old bells cast into a peal of six bells by subscription. Captain S. Penfold and
   Thomas Charles collectors. R.C. 1749 Recast in memory of Patrick and Ellen Ogilvie
   1918.
6. The Rev. John Sutton. John Horn. George Binsted churchwardens. R.C. 1749
   Recast 1952 by public subscription. Mears and Stainbank London.

The old knell was adapted to a sixth bell and until the early years of this century it was rung at 9 a.m. on the day of a funeral. It was rung thus: 'Three strokes on each bell in the following order: 2nd, 4th, Tenor, Treble and 3rd. Then nine, seven or five strokes on the 5th bell for a man, woman or child. Then pull up and let down the Tenor bell'.

These new bells had a narrow escape from destruction by fire, for once more the inhabitants of the High Street heard the dread cries of 'Fire!' and, looking up towards the church, they saw smoke rising from the top of the tower. This fire, it seems, occurred in 1788 and extensively damaged the upper portion of the tower. The bells were either saved or, more likely, their frame withstood the assault of the flames. The tower was rebuilt by Thomas Sueter, one of the famous Hambledon cricketers, and Richard Flood, and there is a stone set into one of the internal walls which is inscribed: 'Thos. Sueter and Richd. Flood; builders A.D.1788'. Also just visible among other names incised in the south-east corner is that of J. Nyren—of whom more in a later chapter.

By the year 1772, the 22nd year of King George III's reign, the American colonies had been lost. It was not long after 1782 that 750 male and female convicts with cattle, seeds and agricultural implements were on their way to Botany Bay, Australia. By 1782 the greatest Englishman who ever served India, Warren Hastings, had saved the British Empire there, and in Sierra Leone a group of philanthropists were on the point of establishing another colony, primarily for freed slaves.

Little Hambledon basked in the glory of its famous cricket club, which in 1782 had just moved its headquarters from Broadhalfpenny to Windmill Down. But the summer of 1782 was a time many Hambledonians were to remember for another reason.

One Wednesday evening in the August of that year Mr. James Stares of Soberton walked to Hambledon with a light heart and step. He was due to meet a friend at the *New Inn* who had some money for him. Who his friend was, how much money was involved and for what services or wager the money changed hands we no longer know. We only know that this meeting was the fateful means of setting the scene for stark, unpremeditated murder.

A little while before, 22-year-old John Taylor, equally light of heart and step, had also set out for the *New Inn*. He lived with his mother beyond Hoe Cross, about

* Robert Catlin

27   The *New Inn*, *c*.1920. The *Bell Inn*, pulled down in the 1920s, is in the background.

half-way between Hambledon and Soberton, and worked at the forge by Cams Corner; of his father we know nothing. Neither do we know the real reason why he also made his way to the *New Inn*. Let us say, for the sake of providing a *raison d'être*, that he was going to see the kitchen maid with whom he was wildly, passionately in love—so blindly that he believed her equally in love with him. As he walked down the village in his clean round frock, he rehearsed rough little speeches which he hoped were both charming and seductive, and revelled inwardly in the yielding replies his imagination placed on her lips.

When he arrived he was hot and thirsty. He had some ale and forgot his rehearsed overtures. When at last he found himself alone with his girl in the kitchen, he was not long in discovering that she had not even remembered the last time they had danced round the maypole, and slowly the dull realisation that he meant nothing to her spread from the pit of his stomach to his heart. It was at that moment, through a hatch to an adjoining room, that he saw Mr. James Stares receive his bag of money. (In 1971, when the first edition of this book was published, the little room where James Stares received his money was still there, but in recent years the wall, with the hatch, separating it from the old bar was removed to enlarge what is now the public bar.)

Stares was not mean. He bought some beer for himself and his friend and later for young Taylor who had joined them and was evidently in need of cheering up. Soon the inn started filling up; Stares continued to enjoy himself until about half past eleven, when he finally rose to go. Taylor, in better spirits, now got up too. As he lived half-way between the inn and Stares' house, he offered to accompany him part of the way home. So it was, some time before midnight, that the two men, slightly drunk, set off together in the darkness, Taylor taking with him the handle of an old mop as a walking stick.

In the cool night air Taylor grew morose again. Conversation soon gave way to silence. As he passed familiar objects along the road and up the footpath leading behind the *Green Man Inn* towards Soberton, the pretty little speeches he had rehearsed that afternoon came back to him mockingly. In silence they climbed the steep slope that led to and round the northern edge of the copse known as Boarhuts (pronounced Borrits). To their right a meadow lay between them and a deep wood, over which a half moon cast a dim light. Ahead, the path led to the lane that joined Hambledon to Hoe Cross and Soberton, and to their left the trees of Boarhuts stood like dark sentinels in the night; not a suspicion of a breeze rustled their leaves. The absolute stillness of this August night was broken only by the men's footsteps and the occasional deep hoot of a distant tawny owl. Suddenly, hearts pounding, both men halted in their tracks; a soft, ascending wheezy cry followed by a shriek rent the air above them as a great white object flapped out of a tree. Together they watched the barn owl glide towards Hoe Cross Farm. Behind them, easily distinguished from its sister constellations, the Great Plough dipped towards the north.

At the point where the footpath joined the lane to Hoe Cross, John Taylor looked quickly behind him and then with a swift, savage stroke he struck Stares across the back of his head with the mop handle. Before James Stares could recover from this unexpected blow, Taylor struck him again with such force that the handle broke; whereupon he thrust the jagged end into Stares' face and continued to rain blows and thrusts at his victim until he had but a foot of crimsoned pole left in his hand and James Stares lay unconscious on the ground. A sadistic lust overcame Taylor. Drawing a knife from his pocket he bent over the dark form lying in the lane.

The moon finally disappeared behind a horizon of treetops; constellation after constellation, star by star paled before the first fingers of early dawn. Shortly after the sun rose behind Boarhuts Copse, James Stares was found. Dark dried blood covered a multiplicity of cuts and bruises on his head, his throat had been cut from ear to ear and again from the point of the chin downwards. He had clearly been robbed of everything he possessed; even the buckles had been cut from his shoes and the buttons from his sleeves. Around him lay the shattered pieces of a stout mop handle.

Suspicion at once fell upon John Taylor, and when he was later apprehended the *Hampshire Chronicle* blandly reported, '... and the tremor he was in upon the occasion very plainly indicated his guilt'.

He was asked for the round frock he had been wearing when he met James Stares at the *New Inn*, but he positively denied having worn one. His mother's house was searched for it, but in vain. It was, however, found later behind the forge in his shop, covered with blood. Taylor was then taken to the Court House where he was further questioned, and during this examination he was ordered to put on his round frock. Mr. Tribe, the master of the *New Inn*, and his maidservant swore it was the same frock they had seen him wearing on that fateful Wednesday evening. But the blacksmith

28   Harry Lott shoeing a horse from Chidden Farm in 1906. This forge at Cams Corner
is near the site of John Taylor's shop.

persisted in denying that the frock was his; he said that he had never had one like it and
had never seen this one before in his life. Finally, in a hushed moment, the wretched
man's mother, who was present, was put on oath and asked whether it was her son's
frock or not. Tearful, shocked and stunned by all that had happened so suddenly to
upheave the course of her uneventful life, she remained silent. The question was put to
her again. She lowered her head and in a whisper scarcely audible, she acknowledged
that it was her son's. Taylor was then committed to stand his trial at the next assizes.

During the first week of March 1783, at the close of the Winchester Assizes, John
Taylor was found guilty of murder and was ordered for execution, 'his body to be
dissected and anatomised'. Also ordered for execution were John Godfrey for murder,
and John Tatterson, Theophilus Crimpey and James Dennison for assaulting and robbing
two men on the highway near Wymering. A number of others were 'sentenced to death'
for robbery and assault, one for burglary, one for stealing a bay gelding and another
for stealing one ewe sheep.

At the scene of this murder, near the top of Cams Hill, where the lane takes a
sharp turn to the left, there stands today the 'murderstone', a simple headstone from
which the fields on either side of the lane take their name. There used to be an inscription
on the stone which began: 'Let future generations know ...' but time and nature—
assisted, it is said, by the Taylor family's hand—have scored these words from view
with truly remarkable thoroughness.

The Cottage of Mr Carter. who made the dressing tables.

Chapter Nine

Moment of Glory - I

The story of Hambledon's moment of glory is the story of a cricket club. Its origin is shrouded in uncertainty; it was all but dissolved in 1771; and then for nearly twenty years it regularly attracted thousands of men, women and children, great and small, famous and unknown, noble and poor to its remote playing fields on Broadhalfpenny and Windmill Downs. After its day was over, it drew about it a cloak of romantic prose, legend, song and poetry that was to set upon it the seal of immortality.

In the days when Aethelgarde was granted the lands of Chidden, Saxon boys in Hamelanduna and other villages all over the country had been playing games with a ball and a cricc (staff or rod) for as long as anyone could recall. From such humble beginnings many games gradually evolved and cricket was one of them. By the time the Tudors came to rule England these games were so popular that the standard of archery had become unacceptably low due to lack of practice. In Henry VIII's reign (1509-1547) cricket, among other activities, was made illegal by Act of Parliament, 'in consequence of crafty persons having invented new and crafty games by reason whereof archery is sore decayed'. This act was not repealed until 1845, so cricket was still technically a banned game throughout the entire period of Hambledon's greatness and for the first 58 years in the life of the M.C.C.

Despite Henry VIII's defence measure, a certain John Derrick of Guildford and his school-fellows of the Free School indulged in 'Crecket and other plaies' about the year 1550. Over a hundred years later, in 1662, some parishioners of Boxgrove, West Sussex, were in serious trouble for playing cricket in their churchyard on a Sunday in May—and moreover, playing in such a violent manner that 'they used to breake the church windows with the ball and a little childe had the like to have her braynes beaten out with a cricket batte'.

In the early 18th century great cricket was being played in Kent, Surrey, Sussex and London. The famous Kent v. All England match played on the Artillery Ground in 1744, watched by the Prince of Wales, his brother 'Butcher' Cumberland and Admiral Vernon among other distinguished spectators, took place before anyone had ever heard of the Hambledon Cricket Club.

What then, one might ask, did this club achieve? In a sentence, Hambledon raised cricket from a sport to an art.

We cannot be sure when the Hambledon Cricket Club was founded, largely due to the loss of the early records in a fire at Lord's. Some cricket historians say that a club must have been formed in the early years of the 18th century, but it is more generally believed to have been about 1750. It is possible that Thomas Land, who moved into Park House in 1759, had already taken over the patronage of the Hambledon Club. The earliest surviving record of cricket at Hambledon dates from 1756. Oddly enough it comes from a passage in the *Reading Mercury* which advertised the loss of a dog at a cricket match on Broadhalfpenny Down on 18 August. In that year, 1756, Hambledon had a team good enough to meet Dartford, who had a formidable side, on the Artillery Ground in London. Then we hear nothing of the club until 1764, when a match was played between Chertsey and 'Hambledon in Hants, called Squire Lamb's [Land's?] club'.

In 1767 Thomas Land died and the Rev. Charles Powlett, who came to the area in 1763, assumed responsibility for the club. He was the illegitimate son of the third Duke of Bolton and Lavinia Fenton—the much admired actress who played the part of Polly Peachum in the first production of John Gay's *The Beggar's Opera*. That same year, 1767, Hambledon won two matches by the huge margins of 262 and 224 'notches', and in the following year the village challenged Kent and beat them easily.

29   The Hambledon team in a cricket match organised by the author's father in 1931 against H.M.S. *Nelson*. Philip Goldsmith is second from the right in the front row.

1769 was not a happy year for the club and a run of misfortune continued into the following season. Fate appeared to have turned her back on Hambledon; patrons and supporters started to resign. The flow of resignations and the run of bad luck continued into 1771, when by mid-season the remaining members were faced with seemingly unavoidable disaster. As the end approached, they met to decide whether or not the club should be dissolved.

It is difficult to understand why the Hambledon Club had been so unsuccessful, for in 1769 it numbered among its players Richard Nyren, George Leer, John Small, Peter Stewart, Thomas Sueter and William Barber, all of whom played regularly for the club at the height of its fame, and also Thomas Ridge and William Hogsflesh, both of whom played until 1775. Not a great deal of information is available about the matches played in these years, but in 1769 Hambledon beat Caterham in August by four wickets and in September by an innings and 41 notches, both handsome margins. In August 1771, Hambledon was soundly beaten by All England at Guildford, losing by 10 wickets. It is said that thousands of pounds were won and lost on this occasion—much of it on side bets.

This may point to the underlying reason for the crisis being, perhaps, less to do with the players' fortune on the field as with the members' fortunes in uncertain bets. Owing to the loss of the old papers at Lord's, we do not know who those members were that met in the clubroom of the *Bat and Ball Inn* on Broadhalfpenny Down late in the 1771 season to decide upon the fate of their club. Some there were who advocated cutting their losses and dissolving the club, but the Rev. Charles Powlett, Philip Dehany, John Richards (of Whitedale, Hambledon) and Richard Nyren must have spoken out against this course. In the end they prevailed, the members agreeing to try their fortunes just once more. Anxious days must have followed before the last opportunity came for turning the club's fortunes. The club were to play Surrey on the Laleham Burway ground at Chertsey on 23 September 1771.

The purse for this historic match was relatively small—a mere £50. The teams were very evenly matched. The Surrey team had £50 to win, side bets apart, and little to lose, whereas for Hambledon their very existence depended upon victory. Imagine their horror, when in the field at a very finely balanced point in the game they observed one of the best Surrey batsmen, Thomas White, making his way to the wicket bearing a bat six inches wide, virtually the width of the stumps. This, in 1771, was unusual but not illegal. In the event White (known as 'Shock' on account of his hair) did not make a great score. Perhaps he was tricked by one of Nyren's 'provokingly deceitful' deliveries and sent up a catch. The result of the match—a win for Hambledon by a single notch.

Immediately on their return to Hambledon the team's captain, principal bowler and batsman drew up the following document:

> In view of the performance of Mr. White of Ryegate on September 23rd that ffour
> and quarter inches shall be the breadth [of a bat] forthwith ----
> This 25th day of September 1771.
> Richard Nyren
> T. Brett
> J. Small

Although this document would not have had the force of law it was generally accepted, complied with and eventually embodied in the laws of the game. Shortly afterwards the club produced an iron frame of sufficient width to admit a cricket bat of the correct size and through which any suspect bat had to pass.

So the club was saved. From the following year until 1796 when it finally broke up, they played 39 matches against All England, winning 23 and drawing one; 19 matches against Kent, winning nine and tying one, with one result unrecorded; and 12 matches against Surrey, winning four and drawing one. They also played 12 single wicket games against All England and Kent, winning seven of them, and in addition they played 105 recorded minor matches.

Club days continued as before on Tuesdays, Hambledon's market day. These were the occasions for the meeting of members in the clubroom at the *Bat and Ball*, and for the players to practise on the Down, where, especially at the height of the club's fame, they would be closely watched by some hundreds of spectators.

The season always started on the first Tuesday in May, and the first meeting was always advertised well in advance in the local papers. On Monday 27 April 1772,— the year Warren Hastings became Governor of Bengal and Captain Cook completed his second voyage round the world—the *Salisbury Journal* announced, 'Hambledon: The first meeting of the Gentlemen of Hambledon Club will be held at Broadhalfpenny, on Tuesday the 5th of May next, at which every subscriber is requested to attend'.

30 'Pitching the Wicket' for an 18th-century-style match at cricket on Broadhalfpenny Down. Lieutenant White, the Captain of H.M.S. *Nelson*'s team, is on the left, Mr. Edward Whalley-Tooker, the Hambledon Captain, is on the right and Philip Goldsmith is about to place the bail. Over 5,000 people watched this match.

By noon on Tuesday 5 May 1772, the players had arrived on the Down. Then, with Richard Nyren moving among them, two teams were picked and the season's first practice game began. Small knots of spectators soon formed round the ground, while within the sound of ball on bat and the cheers of the onlookers for a good hit or a brilliant piece of fielding, the members of the club present—usually a very disappointing number—would retire to the clubroom in the *Bat and Ball Inn*.

In 1772, on the playing fields of Broadhalfpenny, the Artillery Ground, Guildford and Bishopsbourne, the Hambledon men tasted the first heady draught of substantial success against England and Kent. Such a match was played on Broadhalfpenny Down on 23, 24 and 25 June 1772, against England. The match was played for 500 guineas and won by Hambledon by 53 notches.

HAMBLEDON			ENGLAND		
(with Yalden and Edmeads)					
T.Brett	11	2	T. White	35	6
W. Yalden	5	9	J. Fuggles	5	12
J. Small	78	34	Minshull	16	1
T. Sueter	2	9	J. Miller	11	0
R. Nyren	9	4	Gill	5	2
G. Leer	1	0	Palmer	13	8
J. Edmeads	0	6	T. May	15	18
P. Stewart	12	11	Childs	2	0
E. Aburrow	27	0	J. Frame	2	4
W. Hogsflesh	0	4	Lumpy	5	7
W. Barber	1	0	R. May	0	5
Total	146	79	**Total**	109	63

In the same year, the business in the clubroom was, on the whole, dull. Eight new members were elected, including Lord Palmerston, the father of the Prime Minister-to-be, and Bysshe Shelley, the grandfather of the poet, and a Wine cistern was ordered. (Throughout the minutes of these meetings Wine was almost invariably spelt with a capital W.)

There has always been doubt about the exact date of the composition of the Cricket Songs. The one in praise of the men of Hambledon and the other, virtually the same but with the names of the famous players of Kent, are both attributed to the Rev. Reynell Cotton. There are some cricket historians who believe that it was in about 1777 that Cotton resurrected the song he wrote in 1772 to commemorate a Kent victory over Hambledon, but substituted the best-known Hambledon names.

Recent research seems to suggest that the original song was the pro-Hambledon version and that it had been written in the autumn of 1771, presumably to celebrate the survival of Hambledon cricket after the bleak years of 1769 and 1770 when the club was on the brink of dissolution. If this was the case the 'other' version, which first appeared in the *Kentish Gazette* in August 1772 with the Kent names, was probably borrowed and 'adapted' by an unknown hand. It could hardly have been the work of Reynell Cotton who, in May 1773, was 'desired to accept the office of President [of the Hambledon Club] for the ensuing year'. The song was officially published by order of the Hambledon Club in 1781 and later, in July 1790, it was 'Ordered that Mr. Cotton's Song be Framed & glazed and hung up in the Cricket Club Room, & one Hundred Copys are printed'. Its better-known verses have found their way into all books on 18th-century cricket and into most programmes of festival cricket matches held in modern times on Broadhalfpenny Down. It was set to the tune of *King John and the Abbot of Canterbury*, and the words are as follows:

Cricket

Assist, all ye Muses, and join to rehearse
An old English sport, never praised yet in verse;
'Tis Cricket I sing, of illustrious fame,
No nation e'er boasted so noble a game.
Derry down, down, down, derry down.

Great Pindar has bragg'd of his heroes of old—
Some were swift in the race, some in battle were bold;
The brows of the victors with olives were crown'd:
Hark! they shout, and Olympia returns the glad sound.
Derry down, down, down, derry down.

What boasting of Castor and Pollux his brother—
The one famed for riding, for boxing the other;
Compared with our heroes, they'll shine not at all;
What were Castor and Pollux to Nyren and Small?
Derry down, down, down, derry down.

Here's guarding and catching, and throwing and tossing,
And bowling and striking, and running and crossing;
Each mate must excel in some principal part:
The Pentathlon of Greece could not show so much art.
Derry down, down, down, derry down.

The parties are met, and array'd all in white,
Famed Elis ne'er boasted so pleasing a sight;
Each nymph looks askew at her favourite swain,
And views him half stripped both with pleasure and pain.
Derry down, down, down, derry down.

The wickets are pitched now, and measured the ground,
Then they form a large ring, and stand gazing around;
Since Ajax fought Hector, in sight of all Troy,
No contest was seen with such fear and such joy.
Derry down, down, down, derry down.

Ye bowlers take heed, to my precepts attend:
On you the whole fate of the game must depend;
Spare your vigour at first, now exert all your strength,
But measure each step, and be sure pitch a length.
Derry down, down, down, derry down.

Ye strikers observe, when the foe shall draw nigh,
Mark the bowler advancing with vigilant eye;
Your skill all depends upon distance and sight,
Stand firm to your scratch, let your bat be upright.
Derry down, down, down, derry down.

Ye fieldsmen look sharp, lest your pains ye beguile;
Move close like an army, in rank and in file;
When the ball is returned, back it sure, for I trow
Whole states have been ruined by one overthrow.
Derry down, down, down, derry down.

And now the game's o'er, Io victory rings,
Echo doubles her chorus, and Fame spreads her wings;
Let's now hail our champions, all steady and true,
Such as Homer ne'er sung of, nor Pindar e'er knew.
Derry down, down, down, derry down.

Buck, Curry and Hogsflesh, and Barber and Brett,
Whose swiftness in bowling was ne'er equalled yet;
I had almost forgot, they deserve a large bumper,
Little George, the long stop and Tom Sueter, the stumper.
Derry down, down, down, derry down.

Then why should we fear either Sackville or Mann,
Or repine at the loss of both Bayton or Land?
With such troops as these we'll be lords of the game,
Spite Minshull and Miller, and Lumpy and Frame.
Derry down, down, down, derry down.

Then fill up your glass, he's the best who drinks most.
Here's the Hambledon Club!—who refuses the toast?
Let's join in the praise of the bat and the wicket,
And sing in full chorus the patrons of cricket.
Derry down, down, down, derry down.

When we've played our last game, and our fate shall draw nigh
(For heroes of cricket, like others, must die),
Our bats we'll resign, neither troubled nor vexed,
And give up our wickets to those that come next.
Derry down, down, down, derry down.

by the Rev. Mr. Cotton of Winchester

'Buck', (of the *Green Man*), was the dapper Peter Stewart; 'Curry' was Edward Aburrow, also a Hambledon man, whose nickname may have been derived from his reddish hair and temperament to match. Hogsflesh, Barber and Brett, the bowlers, we shall soon meet. 'Little George' was George Leer, the longstop, who, with Tom Sueter the wicket-keeper, must have led the singing of this song so many times from various club rooms after the stumps were drawn.

Sackville was the family name of the Duke of Dorset who, with Sir Horace Mann, Minshull, Miller, Lumpy Stevens and Frame, led the stars of Hambledon's opponents.

Bayton and Land have, in the past, been described as members who had 'deserted' the club. A fairer picture emerges if we give the word 'repine', in the third verse from the end, its more archaic meaning of 'mourn' or 'grieve for'. It is not known who Bayton was, but Land was probably the Land of Park House who was patron of the club before the Rev. Charles Powlett.

In the late October of 1772, when the trees were aflame in their autumn colours and the evenings were drawing in, readers of the local papers and the *St. James Chronicle* may have read: 'The Gentn. of Broadhalfpenny Cricket Club are desired to meet at Dick Nyren's at the George at Hambledon on Saturday the 7th of November on Special Business. N.B. Dinner on Table 3 o'clock'.

The 'annual' or 'general' meeting was always held at the *George Inn*—usually, in the later days of the club, on a moonlit night. The insistence of these final meetings of the year being held on a night on which a moon might be expected (the advertisements in the papers often added after the advertised date 'it being a moon lit night', and the date of one annual meeting was changed so that it would coincide with a full moon), might lead one to imagine that the members indulged in good food, Wine and song, and later in carousal with the pretty girls of the village—but such romantic notions were not the general case. The mundane reason was that the members, many of whom came

31 The saddlery at the bottom of the High Street *c*.1895. Mr. W. Knight stands between his sons. In 1857 this property was owned by Edward Aburrow, the son of the Hambledon Club player nicknamed 'Curry'. Later it became a café, known as the Copper Kettle, but is now a private house.

from afar, preferred to travel home by the light of the moon, which made the journey safer and more pleasant than by no moon at all.

Who was this master of the *George*, servant of cricket and General of Hambledon— Richard Nyren? He was a well-known figure around the village, five feet nine inches tall, very stout but remarkably active. He belonged to an old yeoman family and had for several years been the landlord of the *Bat and Ball Inn*, but in 1772 he had moved down to the *George* in the heart of the village. His whole life was directed to the service of cricket. He was the best all-round player of his day, and with Thomas Brett, a farmer from nearby Catherington, was one of the principal bowlers. Brett, in his prime, was considered the fastest and straightest bowler ever known. Many a bruise welled up beneath the hose of a luckless batsman who mistimed a stroke against him, for a ball from Brett was described as having the force of point-blank shot. Nyren was left-handed and matched Brett's fury by art and cunning, always to a length. His devotion to the game, experience, judgement and knowledge were such that he soon became the accepted captain of all matches; in addition he was always consulted on any matter of precedent or law. He must have been a man of remarkably fine character and judgement, for exception was never taken to his decisions and they were never reversed. He was uncompromising and independent, and could differ with a superior—occasionally holding an opinion with great firmness against the Duke of Dorset—without loss of dignity on either side; yet his success never turned his head or swerved him from his avowed position as the servant of cricket.

During the following year, 1773, defeat followed defeat on the cricket field, but in the clubroom those members who attended did much work, under their newly elected president for the year, the Rev. Reynell Cotton.

The first matter to be dealt with after the preliminaries was Wine (with a capital W again). It was decided that the club should pay William Barber's Wine licence. Barber was now the landlord of the *Bat and Ball* and a competent bowler for Hambledon; he and William Hogsflesh of Southwick were the two change bowlers for the early Hambledon teams. Barber also performed many other useful jobs for the club such as rolling and repairing the ground, collecting and returning empty bottles, arranging certain dinners, collecting subscriptions and checking the bills of the players before presenting them to the stewards. In addition he arranged dinners on his own behalf on both Broadhalfpenny Down and distant grounds. These he used to advertise in the *Hampshire Chronicle*, as on 25 August 1775, when that newspaper carried the following paragraph:

> Barber from Broadhalfpenny will pitch several tents on the Down, where Wines and Provisions of all Sorts may be had at the most reasonable Rates, and the Ladies who honour him with their Company will be as much at their Ease as if they were in their own Dressing Room.

Richard Nyren also used to have refreshment booths on the ground and on occasion they would advertise together: 'Ladies and Gentlemen will find an excellent cold collation everyday on the Down at Nyren and Barber's Booths'.

32 The Hambledon team arriving at Broadhalfpenny in Tom Parker's coach and four for a cricket match with the Ancient Mariners from H.M.S. *Mercury*, arranged by the author in 1951.

But to return to the clubroom. Having, at the first meeting in May 1773, agreed on Barber's Wine licence, the assembled members at subsequent meetings that year decided that a Pipe of Wine (a large cask holding 105 gallons) be sent for from Mr. Smith of Winton, for the use of the club, and that a bin should be built in Barber's cellar at the expense of the club. It also ordered that Barber should 'take care that the Down is repaired'.

As the expense of conveying the players, umpire and scorer to distant playing fields had for some time been worrying John Richards, the treasurer, it was possibly he who suggested buying a vehicle for this purpose. On 25 May 1773 it was agreed that 'Mr. Richards do endeavour to find out the Expense of A Machine to Convey the Cricketers to distant parts and to report the same next meeting'. By 17 August there were still differences of opinion on the subject, but it was agreed 'on A Ballot that Mr. Richards shall pay for the Machine to carry the Cricketers out of the Surplus Money of the Subscription to the Club'.

The time of pitching the wickets for practice matches having been brought forward to half past ten, it was agreed that the players who arrived after eleven o'clock were to be fined threepence, which was to be spent on punch for those who had arrived punctually.

The players were paid, but at this date, 1773, we do not know how much. It was probably about three shillings or two shillings and sixpence per match or game. In 1782 this was increased to four shillings if winners and three shillings if losers, provided they were on the ground ready to play by the appointed time.

If they lived too far away to walk to the ground, their travelling expenses were also paid. Each case was considered by the club members present. On 17 August 1773, it was agreed that James Bayley, who is believed to have come from Mitcham near Wimbledon, should be allowed the expense of his horse-hire when he came to practise on Tuesdays.

At the Annual Meeting on 1 October 1773, held as usual at the *George Inn*, the old ever-sore question of non-payment of subscriptions arose, as it was to arise again and again through the years. Lastly Mr. H. Bonham and the Rev. Charles Powlett were asked to become stewards for the year 1774.

On the field that year good fortune once again attended the players, their greatest victory being the defeat of England at Broadhalfpenny by an innings and 52 runs on 22, 23 and 24 June. (*Scores and Biographies* erroneously places this match on the Laleham Burway Ground.)

ENGLAND			HAMBLEDON CLUB	with Lumpy
Duke of Dorset	19	6	E. Aburrow	9
Earl of Tankerville	18	35	J. Small, sen	47
— Stone Esq.	14	4	Lumpy	22
— Minshull	37	38	G. Leer	12
— May	7	6	T. Sueter	67
J. Miller	3	26	R. Nyren	21
— Wood	10	0	J. Aylward	37
T. White	5	0	R. Francis	29
— Palmer	0	6	P. Stewart	11
— Childs	2	6	R. Purchase	37
W. Yalden	1	0	T. Brett	9
Byes	6	6	Byes	6
Total	122	133		307

(This is the first recorded occasion where a single innings exceeded 300 runs.)

In the clubroom the members achieved some good work, even managing to collect some subscriptions in arrears. However, this year was chiefly important for the special committee formed to review and co-ordinate the laws of the game. Already committees of the Hambledon Club had passed certain laws regulating the width of the bat and weight of the ball, and such was their prestige that these rulings were widely accepted. On 25 February 1774 a committee of noblemen and gentlemen of Kent, Hampshire, Surrey, Sussex, Middlesex and London met at the *Star and Garter*, Pall Mall, and there they revised and recorded 'The Laws of the Noble Game of Cricket'. Representing

Hambledon at this meeting were Philip Dehany, the Rev. Charles Powlett and Charles Coles.

Subsequently smaller committees or a 'council of the Hambledon Club' were created to settle a precedent, review a law or decide upon a point of issue such as the legality of throwing as opposed to bowling or the size of the wicket and so on.

In the clubroom at Broadhalfpenny it was agreed this year (1774) to allow Richard Purchase, a blacksmith who lived at Liss, two shillings and sixpence for the hire of his horse on practice days. Purchase first played for Hambledon against England in the unsuccessful year of 1773. He was known in later life as 'old Doctor Purchase' because he occasionally used to bleed the villagers. He was a slowish bowler keeping a good length, a fair hitter and a 'tolerable' field.

33 The Hambledon Men and the Ancient Mariners around the Commemorative Stone in 1951. The author is standing in the centre, fourth from the left, pipe in hand.

In 1774 the members of the Hambledon team were rising to their prime, yet within ten years they were to be soundly beaten by those they were now teaching, a team that included two of their own sons. And a few years later they were to be dubbed 'the old rear guard'. Of these we have already met the bowlers Richard Nyren and Brett, Barber and Hogsflesh and also John Bayley and 'Doctor' Purchase. The bowling of the 1770s was all underarm and generally considered to have been pretty soft, but such was not necessarily the case. Brett bowled with considerable fire, and a certain Browne of Brighton is said to have had a delivery so fast that on one occasion he beat the batsman, wicket-keeper and longstop, and killed a dog among the spectators.

But now to the batsmen of the Hambledon Club. John Small was perhaps the greatest of them all in those early days around 1774. He was originally a shoemaker, but later devoted his whole life to cricket, playing in the great matches and making bats and balls which the club bought from him. The value of a bat in those days was about two shillings and sixpence, and a ball would be worth about three shillings and six-pence. Not only was John Small a superb batsman but he was the first to make short hits pay, being a perfect judge of the short run. He was also a splendid fieldsman, always playing middle wicket, and was almost as knowledgeable about the finer points of the game and its laws as was Nyren himself.

He was a very accomplished musician, playing both the violin and 'cello, and for 75 years was a member of the Petersfield choir. There was an oft-told story that on his way to a musical party he was crossing a field 'when a vicious bull made at him. Our hero, with the characteristic coolness and presence of mind of a good cricketer began playing upon his bass, to the admiration and perfect satisfaction of the mischievous beast'. This story clearly lost nothing in its telling through the years, with its image of an Orpheus-like cricketer standing with his 'bass' before a bull reminiscent of Ferdinand beneath his cork tree. In truth there was probably a stout fence between them.

Tom Sueter was a Hambledon man, a carpenter and builder. He was a hard-hitting left-handed batsman and one of the first to move out of his crease towards the ball. He was also the best wicket-keeper of his day, one who would frequently stump a man out against Brett's tremendous bowling. He had a very fine tenor voice and sang in the Hambledon choir; when he died he left a sovereign in order that an anthem might be sung at his funeral. 'With what rapture,' wrote John Nyren, 'have I hung upon his notes when he gave us a hunting song in the clubroom after a day's practice was over.'

George Leer was another Hambledon man. At least he was born and buried at Hambledon but, cricket apart, he earned his living as a brewer in nearby Petersfield. Unequalled in the all-important position of longstop—for the wicket-keeper of those days wore no gloves or pads—he could cover an enormous amount of ground against the swiftest bowling ever known. He also had a good counter-tenor voice, frequently joining Tom Sueter and John Small in music after a game.

In those times, the day's pleasure never ended with the drawing of the stumps, for Wine and song always completed a day's cricket. Over countless cricket grounds in Sussex, Surrey, Kent, Middlesex and Hampshire a chorus of men's voices would ring out from brightly lit clubrooms over darkening pitches. Of these moments and of Leer's and Sueter's glees at the *Bat and Ball* in particular, John Nyren (who was no mean musician himself) wrote:

> I have been there, and still would go:
> 'Twas like a little heaven below.

The Snowdrop Field Hambledon

Chapter 10

Moment of Glory - II

For the Hambledon Cricket Club the 1775 season started, as so often the season did, with a single wicket match. This game was played on the Artillery Ground between five Hambledon men and five of Kent. Small, Brett, Sueter, Leer and White played for Hambledon, while the star of their opponents was the formidable bowler Edward Stevens, much better known as 'Lumpy'. It is generally believed that the wicket of those days consisted of two stumps, one foot high and two feet apart, surmounted by a bail, but evidence from that time is confused. Many historians challenge these dimensions and they probably varied from club to club. Nevertheless, whatever the dimensions, the wicket at this match was of two stumps.

There was a great deal of money wagered and Hambledon, after their success during the previous year, was heavily favoured. This meant that when the last Hambledon man went in to bat there were a number of anxious men among the spectators, for there were fourteen runs to make. Not only those with money staked but the whole ground—thousands of spectators—were hushed and tense. The batsman was John Small, one of the finest of his day, and the bowler was 'Lumpy', who was at that time second to none. In this battle of the gods Small made his runs, but it took him two and three quarter hours to do so, and during that time Lumpy bowled the ball clean through his wicket three times without dislodging the bail.

After the match the Duke of Dorset sent John Small a present of a fine violin and paid the carriage. Small returned the compliment by sending His Grace two bats and balls, also paying the carriage. But the match gave the Hambledon Club something to think about. It was blatantly unfair that a bowler's straightest balls should, having beaten the batsman, be unrewarded. A committee decided that a third stump ought to be added, though there were many who thought that this would ruin the game. The improvement was gradually adopted and became general by about 1780. However, before this date the best balls of the new 'length' bowlers had been passing over the

87

bail, and this had already resulted in an increase in the height of the wicket. So, by 1780 the wicket consisted of three stumps 22 ins. by 6 ins. (In 1814 their height and width were increased to 26 ins. by 8 ins. and in 1817 to their present dimensions of 27 ins. by 8 ins.)

The mantle of greatness that had settled on Hambledon made little difference to the work that went on in the fields, as it had for centuries, but the village thrived on its fame. The thousands who flocked to Broadhalfpenny for the great matches and the hundreds who watched the weekly trial matches brought money with them, and the village prospered. It must have been a very happy place, with stories about the 'Great Ones' circulating of an evening—like another story at Lumpy's expense.

This occurred when one of the great matches finished early in the day. The players were gathered about their tents when a lanky, raw-boned countryman shambled up to them and offered to play any one of them at single wicket for five pounds. It seemed some village idiot had blundered among the gods. Nyren nudged Lumpy, as members and spectators pressed closer to hear what was happening, and told him it would be five pounds easily won. Lumpy was suspicious and hung back despite encouragement shouted from the nearest bystanders. Finally he was persuaded but, cautious as ever, he would only stake one pound of the money himself, the rest being subscribed.

Lumpy, now more confident, made the countryman go in first, intending to bowl him out quickly with one of his famous shooters and then to settle the contest without delay. This great, long fellow took up his stance at the wicket and, having arms like hop-poles, he reached out to all Lumpy's balls, bowl what he might, slashing and thrashing away in the most ludicrous style, sending ball after ball flying all over the field. At length Lumpy got him, but not before he had made a great number of runs.

The great All England bowler now went in, not knowing what to expect. The first ball came at him hard, right along the ground and straight at the wicket. Lumpy managed to stop it. The succeeding balls were all the same—fast, along the ground and straight, and before he could make many runs he was clean bowled. The crowd roared with laughter as the astounded Lumpy stumped back to the other players, swearing he would never play another single match as long as he lived.

1776: another year passed as Hambledon's star still rose towards its zenith. Success on the field predominated, and a ground on Chidden Holt came into use mainly for minor games, though in this year Hambledon suffered a defeat by England in a major match there. In June their fortunes were reversed in a match at Sevenoaks, Kent, where Hambledon scored a total of 325 'notches' or runs to England's 250. All these 'notches' had to be run, for there was no white boundary line; no 'fours' or 'sixes'. One is apt to pity the poor batsmen in those days before boundaries, but fielders had their problems too, such as retrieving a ball hit among the spectators. It was at this Sevenoaks match against England that Francis Booker, fielding at mid wicket, caught out four Hambledon batsmen, and this could well have been the match where he made his famous catch, having first leapt over a fence.

The village continued to prosper and revel in more stories of its new-found greatness. Such a story concerns Peter Stewart, a Hambledon man, a carpenter and

34 Ploughing at Coombe Down, Hambledon, the traditional way.

35 Mr. Valentine Hill ploughing at Hoe Cross Farm in 1920 with a Titan Tractor. He owned Rushmere Farm from 1908 to 1919 and would have known more precisely than we do today what happened to the old farmhouse that disappeared so completely. The young man on the shut-cock plough is David Aldred.

shoemaker by trade, but for some time landlord of the *Green Man Inn*, Hambledon. His nickname was 'Buck' on account of his dapper appearance, and he was the team's humorist. He was travelling once with the rest of the team in the special caravan built to carry them to away matches when it overturned. No one was hurt and the passengers, one by one, crawled out—all that is except Buck, who refused all appeals to help right the vehicle. 'I've just had one good turn over,' he shouted back. 'You just right this here vehicle with me in it, for one good turn deserves another.' This witty repartee, though unlikely to gain high rating in the humour stakes today, was the talk of the village for weeks.

By the end of July this year (1776) it would have been generally known that the 13 American States had declared Independence. On Sunday 8 December Mr. William Stevens, vicar of Hambledon, announced in church, as did bishops, vicars and curates throughout the land, that, by Royal Proclamation, a day of fasting and mourning was to be observed the following Friday 13th because of the country's defeat in North America.

And so to 1777, the year the Hambledon men played their greatest match, when they defeated All England at Sevenoaks by an innings and 168 runs. This match was played with three stumps to the wicket, and finally dispelled any doubts that the game would be unduly shortened by the addition of a third stump.

On Tuesday 17 June the England opening batsmen walked bravely from the edge of the ground, surrounded by spectators, tents and refreshment booths, cast a glance round the field and prepared themselves for Brett's first ball. That same afternoon the last two England batsmen walked back from the pitch to their tents. They were in no way downcast for, although their team's first innings had not lasted long, there had been some good hitting and they had scored 166 runs—a respectable score by any standards. It was not long before the opening pair of Hambledon men took that nerve-wracking walk from pavilion to wicket, and a little after 5 o'clock a Farnham waggoner, on his way east through Sevenoaks paused to watch the play. For half an hour he watched the left-handed batsman, James Aylward, defending his three stumps against the bowling of Lumpy Stevens, and any loose ball from this great bowler was hit in grand style for four or five runs. At length the waggoner managed to tear himself away and continued his journey.

All next day Hambledon batted, James Aylward carrying his bat till the stumps were drawn. On Thursday morning, shortly before noon, the Farnham waggoner on his homeward journey paused again to watch the match. To his astonishment James Aylward was still batting and continued to do so till about three o'clock when he was bowled by Bullen, having made 167 runs, the highest score ever made in the annals of cricket at that time.

Time was getting short when the first England batsmen went in to open their second innings, but Hambledon, despite their great advantage, did not throw away a single chance; they fielded with even greater care than in their first innings, and in consequence their opponents did not score half their previous number of runs.

The score card for this great Hambledon victory reads:

HAMBLEDON CLUB AGAINST ALL ENGLAND

ENGLAND

	1st Innings			2nd Innings	
Duke of Dorset	0	b Brett		5	c Lord Tankerville
Lumpy	1	b Brett		2	Not out
Wood	1	b Brett		1	b Nyren
White	8	c Veck		10	Run out
Miller	27	c Small		23	b Brett
Minchin	60	Not out		12	b Taylor
Bowra	2	b Brett		4	b Taylor
Bullen	13	b Lord Tankerville		2	b Nyren
Booker	8	c Brett		2	b Brett
Yalden	6	c Small		8	c Nyren
Pattenden	38	b Brett		0	c Brett
Byes	2		Byes	0	
Total	166		**Total**	69	

HAMBLEDON

	1st Innings	
Lord Tankerville	3	b Wood
Leer	7	b Wood
Veck	16	b Lumpy
Small	33	c White
Francis	26	c Wood
Nyren	37	b Lumpy
Sueter	46	b Wood
Taylor	32	c Bullen
Aburrow	22	c Minchin
Aylward	167	b Bullen
Brett	9	Not out
Byes	5	
Total	403	

Won by Hambledon by 168 runs in one innings.

As far back as man has records the common lands of Broadhalfpenny Down had grazed sheep and cattle, while its thickets and saplings had provided the inhabitants of Hambledon and Chidden with material to repair or renew their fences. It has always been a bleak spot, swept by rain and wind in winter. In summer it has, over the centuries, basked in glorious isolation amid panoramic views of rolling countryside. We may never understand why, in the mid-18th century, the Hambledon Cricket Club chose this down to be its playing field and headquarters, nor why it rose to such heights of fame, attracting thousands of colourful people to watch the splendid spectacle of 'a match at cricket'.

In the 1770s and early '80s booths would spring up around the ground before an important match. There would be those of Barber and Nyren, and possibly others, selling food and drink. Some of the nobility brought their own tents and had them pitched beside the ground. (Lord Tankerville, a regular player on the Hambledon side, frequently did this.) A tent was pitched for the players, sometimes two—one for each team—and another for the ladies, and most of them flew pennants or flags. In addition a lodge, a semi-permanent structure, was put up at the beginning of each season for the members.

On the day of a great match thousands of spectators (estimated on one occasion as some twenty thousand) would flock to this remote plot of land. Dukes, earls, lords, knights, squires, yeomen and ordinary folk all made their way to Hambledon in coaches and four, caravans, wagons, carts and on horseback. A vast majority came on foot, frequently some considerable distances. Around the ground this colourful and enthusiastic throng would settle down to enjoy a day's cricket.

On the days of the big matches a great deal of money often changed hands. The matches themselves were usually played for £500, but in addition there were always

36 The heart of the village, 1900. The post office, People's Market and *George Inn* where the annual cricket dinners were held in the 18th century. The open ditch, on the right, often overflowed and flooded the road when the springs ran high.

many side wagers, sometimes for vast sums of money. There never seems to have been any sharp practice during this time; it was not until the early 19th century that cricket entered a dark age of crooked dealings and bribery; certainly no such practices would have been tolerated by the Hambledon Club.

John Nyren tells of an occasion when Miller and Minshull, the only batsmen of their time that Hambledon had cause to fear, made so many runs for England that the backers of the Hambledon team edged off all their money and laid it heavily on the opposing side. When at last the England team were out, John Small went in first for Hambledon. Although he was not able to make many runs, he did manage to stay in while five fellow-batsmen came out to join him, only to return whence they had come after a brief, inglorious stay. Finally Richard Nyren went in, and a great partnership and great cricket began. Nyren hit 98 runs and Small 110 before they were parted.

As Nyren walked back he received the applause of the crowd, and when he had joined his fellow players the congratulations continued, but one or two members who had shifted their bets to the other side complained, 'You may win your match but we shall lose our money.'

Nyren turned on them shortly. 'Another time,' he said, 'don't bet your money against such men as we.'

So far as statements in published reports are concerned, and they are by no means complete, stake money amounting to £32,527 10s. was involved in Hambledon matches. Of that sum, the club won £22,497 10s. and lost £10,030.

By 1777 Hambledon's fame had spread far and wide; it seemed that nothing could diminish the prowess of the club, and the village revelled in the warm glow of glory. At this point we may leave the 'Old Guard' in undisputed sovereignty, but changes were soon to come as the boys and men they were then teaching reached their standard and surpassed them. In the next few years new names became famous, one by one, and Hambledon's star shone more brightly than ever before.

Noah Mann started playing for the club about 1777. He was an athletic man, a very fast runner and an expert on horseback. He used to ride at least twenty miles every Tuesday to practice, and as he approached the down his friends would throw handkerchiefs on the ground, which he would pick up, stooping from his horse at full gallop.

At one match against All England, Hambledon went in with a large number of runs to get. It was clear to all that there would be a close finish. The opening pair looked most unsure of themselves, and they were both dismissed with a very meagre score in the books. The third batsman fared little better, and Noah Mann pleaded with Richard Nyren to be allowed to go in next and set about this England bowling. The runs came slowly, and as each wicket fell Noah kept worrying Nyren to let him go in, but the Hambledon captain steadfastly refused. Finally the penultimate wicket fell and Noah strode out to the pitch. Ten runs stood between Hambledon and victory.

There was almost complete silence around the ground, the tension all but tangible. Every spectator knew the state of the game, and many thousands of pounds hung on ten runs. Many thousands of supporters, whether they had wagers laid or not, also hung on every movement in the field, the old farmers from all the country around leaning forward on their tall staves. The strain was too much for Sir Horace Mann, one of the great patrons of cricket and godfather to his namesake Noah's youngest son. He had, as usual, a large sum wagered and, as he frequently did when the situation was tense, he walked about outside the ground cutting the daisies down with his stick.

Lumpy's first ball to Noah was straight and swift. Noah stopped it dead. The second ball was the same and this too Noah put down in front of him. Lumpy's third ball was even faster but pitched a little high and Noah, a hard-hitting left-hander, reached out and hit it. Almost simultaneously a great roar rose from the crowd, as much to relieve the tension as to applaud a good hit. Six of the ten were run. Then a tense hush descended on the field again while bowler and batsman pitted their wits and skill against each other, resulting in a breathtaking duel—no runs, no wickets. Finally the runs were made, the match was won. The tension lifted and the spectators turned to each other, joyful or desperate according to their loyalties.

Later Noah upbraided Nyren for not putting him in earlier, but the latter had been right, for he knew Noah to be a man of such nerve and self-possession that the thought of so much depending on him would not have the paralysing effect that it would on many others.

Poor Noah died a tragic death at the age of 33, in December 1789. After a day's shooting he returned to the *Half-Moon Inn* at his native Northchapel, wet and tired. There he drank freely with his friends till physical weariness, alcohol and the pleasant warmth of the room got the better of him. He refused to go home and insisted on sleeping the night in his chair in front of the fire, so his companions left him. During the night when sound asleep he fell into the fire, and before he could save himself his clothes were alight. He was so badly burned that he died the next day.

About 1784 two real rustics, the Walker brothers—Tom and Harry—started playing for the club. They came from Witley in Surrey, Harry the hitter—Harry's half hour was as good as Tom's afternoon—and Tom the stonewaller, nicknamed Old Everlasting. Tom used to grunt when forced by a shooting ball to act quickly, and his grunt was described as being very like that of a broken-winded horse, only a deeper bass.

In 1782 David Harris started playing for the club, and it was not long before he surpassed Brett and Lumpy to become the supreme bowler of his day. He was a potter from Crookham in Hampshire, and his accurate combination of length, speed and leg spin forced batsmen to go forward in defence. He had a distinctive action. He would pause before he started his run, standing fiercely upright, then with a graceful swinging movement of his arm he would bring the ball to his forehead, draw back his right foot and start his run. He reached the wicket at full momentum and released the ball with almost incredible force for an underarm action.

A few years afterwards 'Honest' John Wells and the Beldham brothers, all from Farnham, joined the 'younger set'. William Beldham, later known as Silver Billy, was to become the supreme batsman of his time. Also about this time Richard Nyren's son John, the author of *The Young Cricketer's Tutor* and *The Cricketers of my Time*, started to play for Hambledon, and John Small junior began to eclipse his illustrious father.

These new or second generation players brought Hambledon to the peak of its fortunes, and through them the game itself developed as the skill of its masters increased. The third stump, the increased height of the wicket and the very fast length bowling of Harris, whose balls would rise sharply from the ground, resulted in a great improvement in batsmanship, forcing a manner of forward play unknown to the 'Old Guard'.

Silver Billy in later years spoke scornfully of the batting of the older team, describing them as 'puddling around in their creases'. However the bowlers did not despair but, led by David Harris, improved their own techniques. The ball began to fly from their hands faster and straighter, more constantly to a length, broke and twisted and swerved, rose sharply or kept unexpectedly low, ever seeking to beat the bat and scatter the wicket or at least to rise from the bat to a fieldsman's hands. As a result of this mortal duel between bowler and batsman, the game of cricket rapidly developed in technique, constantly demanding more skill and technical perfection from its players, till it became the art which Hambledon was ultimately to pass on to Lord's and, through the M.C.C., to the cricket-playing world of today.

In 1781 another change occurred, unrelated to the game itself, which poses a riddle. It concerned the standing toasts at club dinners. Up to 1781 the only toasts allowed were 'The King' and 'The President of the Club' (Mr. George Garnier of Rookesbury in 1781). In this year four extra toasts were introduced, and the order in which they were to be drunk was laid down. They were:

1. The Queen's Mother.
2. The King.
3. The Hambledon Club.
4. Cricket.
5. To the Immortal Memory of Madge.
6. The President.

The first toast is a puzzle. In 1761, King George III married Princess Charlotte Sophia of Mecklenburg-Strelitz, whose mother, Princess Albertine Elizabeth, had died earlier that year. It is inconceivable that the Queen's mother had ever heard of Hambledon.

If the apostrophe 's' were absent in the original order, the Queen Mother might have been an honorary title bestowed on Augusta, the widowed Princess of Wales. Her late husband, Frederick Prince of Wales, was interested in cricket; he had been a spectator at the famous Kent v. All England match in 1744 with his brother the Duke of Cumberland. It has also been said that the Prince of Wales had been struck by a cricket ball shortly before his fatal illness. At least here—in more ways than one—is a cricket connection.

If, having rid ourselves of the apostrophe 's', we substitute a hyphen and turn to the Oxford Dictionary we find: 'Queen-Mother: Queen's herb—tobacco. So called after Catherine de Medici to whom it was sent through Nico, the ambassador in Portugal'. So this first toast may have been the signal that dinner was complete and that after-dinner pipes might be lit.

The fifth Toast has, to an even greater extent, exercised the minds of cricket historians over the years. 'To the Immortal Memory of Madge.' Who was Madge?

Was she a favoured maidservant or the young daughter of a player or member who had captured the hearts and imagination of those who knew her? John Nyren would never have missed so human a story.

Was Mr. Madge a legendary player, playing before records were regularly kept—a W.G. Grace of his day? I have never heard of any club that regularly drank to 'The Immortal Memory of Grace'.

A strange clue is given in Darwin's *British Clubs*. Of Hambledon he wrote, '... [the gentlemen] drank a list of six standing toasts, one of which, regrettable to say, was of the most undisguised impropriety'. Was 'madge' a rude word? Reference to Groce's *Dictionary of the Vulgar Tongue*, 1796, gives for madge —'a woman's private parts'. What was the point of such a toast? Why to the *Immortal Memory* of Madge?

The key to this conundrum must lie in the date—1781. Change was in the air. As we have seen, new names were becoming famous, a new style of play was developing, the old two-stump wicket one foot high had given way to the three-stump wicket 22 ins. high (1780); even the playing field and headquarters were to move (1782) from Broadhalfpenny to Windmill Down at the instigation of the Duke of Dorset and others, who found the old ground too remote. No wonder that many of the older members viewed all these changes with an anxious eye. How they must have looked back a decade or two to the old days on the Down, the old team, the old safe, traditional style of play—all symbolised in the old two-stump wicket. If one reflects a moment on the old schoolboy parody:

> The boy stood on the burning deck
> Playing a game of cricket ...

we are indelicately introduced to the male or three-stump wicket; thus the two-stump wicket becomes identifiable as the madge wicket—even just 'Madge'. So the toast to the Immortal Memory of Madge becomes a nostalgic drink to the old days—never to return.

It was in 1782 that the club moved its playing field to Windmill Down, a less bleak spot nearer the village. It made little difference to Hambledon; John Nyren records that it was for the better, being one of the finest places for playing on that he ever saw. Broadhalfpenny's mantle of renown fell easily upon the new playing field, and the colourful, enthusiastic crowds all welcomed the change. It did not, though, go far enough to satisfy the game's need for a more accessible mecca.

Hambledon, in the south of Hampshire, was not an easy place to get to, and in 1787 the Mary-le-Bone Cricket Club was formed in London. Ironically its chief founder was the then President of the Hambledon Club—the Earl of Winchelsea. By the following year this newly-formed club, already attracting many of the chief players and patrons of cricket, had acquired sufficient influence to undertake a revision of the laws. As the importance of the M.C.C. grew, so the great days on Windmill Down became fewer and fewer, and more members resigned. When Richard Nyren left Hambledon in 1791 the old club virtually broke up, but the men of Hambledon seemed reluctant to concede defeat, and the club lingered on for another five years.

To add to Hambledon's misfortunes, war with France broke out in 1793, and many of the club's remaining supporters 'went to sea'. By 1795 there were but 43 gentlemen subscribers, and on the list of these there was noted: 'Captain Calder—gone to sea. Captain Hambleton—gone to sea. The Reverend John Richards [the treasurer's son]—gone abroad. Mr. T. Whalley—gone. The Honourable Mr. Bligh—gone to sea. Lord Seymour—gone to sea. Captain T. Lennox Frederick—gone to sea'. Against Mr. Leigh's name the comment 'gone to the devil' had been inserted, but was later erased. The last entry in the Club's minute book was dated 21 September 1796, and simply records the words—'no gentlemen'.

And so passed Hambledon's moment of glory. It was not derived from its geographical position, its market and fairs or powerful lords of the manor as it might have been, but from the determination of a few men who nurtured a cricket club.

THE YOUNG

CRICKETER'S TUTOR;

COMPRISING

FULL DIRECTIONS FOR PLAYING THE ELEGANT AND
MANLY GAME OF

CRICKET;

WITH A COMPLETE VERSION OF ITS LAWS
AND REGULATIONS:

By JOHN NYREN,

*A Player in the celebrated Old Hambledon Club, and in the
Mary-le-Bone Club.*

TO WHICH IS ADDED,

"𝕿𝖍𝖊 𝕮𝖗𝖎𝖈𝖐𝖊𝖙𝖊𝖗𝖘 𝖔𝖋 𝕸𝖞 𝕿𝖎𝖒𝖊,"

OR,

RECOLLECTIONS OF THE MOST FAMOUS OLD
PLAYERS:

BY THE SAME AUTHOR.

———

THE WHOLE COLLECTED AND EDITED

By CHARLES COWDEN CLARKE.

———

LONDON:

PUBLISHED BY

EFFINGHAM WILSON, ROYAL EXCHANGE.

———

1833.

37   Facsimile from Lucas's *The Hambledon Men.*

Chapter Eleven

Moment of Glory - III

All cricket historians, at some time in their studies, go back to John Nyren's *The Young Cricketer's Tutor*, and a remarkable piece of literature it is. The title page (opposite) suggests that Charles Cowden Clarke merely collected and edited Nyren's writings, and Miss Mary Nyren, the old man's grand-daughter, seems to confirm this theory. 'There is no doubt,' she wrote, 'that John Nyren himself wrote *The Young Cricketer's Tutor* and *The Cricketers of My Time;* Clarke only edited them.' Yet, on the available evidence, it seems Nyren possessed little writing skill—'disappointing in the extreme by any standard,' wrote John Arlott.

On the other hand Mrs. Cowden Clarke, in her *My Long Life,* mentions her husband's share in Nyren's book. She referred to Nyren as 'a vigorous old friend who had been a famous cricketer in his youth and early manhood, and who in his advanced age,* used to come and communicate his cricketing expressions to Charles, with chuckling pride and complacent reminiscence'. She implied that it was her husband who had been responsible for the the writing. But again, the available evidence of his other writings does not support this. Neither of these two extremely pedestrian writers had, individually, produced anything of great merit, anything so fine or truly inspired as their closely collaborated *The Young Cricketer's Tutor* or *The Cricketers of My Time.*

The explanation must be that Nyren, in relating his experiences to Clarke, and looking back over the years through the rose-tinted spectacles of nostalgia, emanated so much romantic enthusiasm that the writer caught it and retained it—recording most of the original words and phrases. Here, to draw to a close Hambledon's Moment of Glory, is the famous 'There was high feasting ...' passage. Imagine Nyren, with 'chuckling pride', relaxing in the company of Cowden Clarke, looking back over several decades and saying:

* John Nyren was 69 years old when *The Young Cricketer's Tutor* was printed.

There was high feasting held on Broad-Halfpenny during the solemnity of one of our grand matches. Oh! it was a heart-stirring sight to witness the multitude forming a complete and dense circle round that noble green. Half the county would be present, and all their hearts with us. Little Hambledon pitted against All England was a proud thought for the Hampshire men. Defeat was glory in such a struggle—Victory, indeed, made us only 'a little lower than angels'. How those fine brawn-faced fellows of farmers would drink to our success! And then, what stuff they had to drink!—Punch!— not your new *Ponche à la Romaine*, or *Ponche à la Groseille*, or your modern cat-lap milk punch—punch be-devilled; but good, unsophisticated John Bull stuff—stark!— that would stand on end—punch that would make a cat speak! Sixpence a bottle! The ale too!—not the modern horror under the same name, that drives as many men melancholy-mad as the hypocrites do; —not the beastliness of these days, that will make a fellow's inside like a shaking bog—and as rotten; but barleycorn, such as would put the souls of three butchers into one weaver. Ale that would flare like turpentine—genuine Boniface!—This immortal viand (for it was more than liquor) was vended at twopence per pint. The immeasurable villainy of our vintners would, with their march of intellect (if ever they could get such a brewing), drive a pint of it out into a gallon. Then the quantity the fellows would eat! Two or three of them would strike dismay into a round of beef. ... There would this company, consisting most likely of some thousands, remain patiently and anxiously watching every turn of fate in the game, as if the event had been the meeting of two armies to decide their liberty. And whenever a Hambledon man made a good hit, worth four or five runs, you would hear the deep mouths of the whole multitude baying away in pure Hampshire—'Go hard!—go hard!—*Tich* and turn!—*tich* and turn!' To the honour of my countrymen, let me bear testimony upon this occasion also, as I have already done upon others. Although their provinciality in general, and personal partialities individually, were naturally interested in behalf of the Hambledon men, I cannot call to recollection an instance of their wilfully stopping a ball that had been hit out among them by one of our opponents. Like *true* Englishmen, they would give an enemy fair play. How strongly are all those scenes, of fifty years bygone, painted in my memory!—and the smell of that ale comes upon me as freshly as the new May flowers.

Whitedale Farm

Chapter Twelve

Decline

The 19th century brought to the privileged of England great splendour and wealth, but to the majority of people it brought bitter class hatred, misery and grinding poverty. Great changes were to come, and in 1800 those changes had already begun to leave their mark upon Hambledon.

Over and over again visitors to the village recorded the same sad story of neglect. Mr. W.R. Weir, one of the many cricket pilgrims who were now visiting the scenes of earlier glory and colourful triumph, wrote:

> My first visit to this classic region was made on foot from London and I remember I experienced something akin to regret for having travelled so far to see so little. The old Bat and Ball Inn, with its dingy signboard creaking on its rusty hinges as the chill October wind swept over the downs, looked very forlorn, while the landlady was as sour as the beer she tendered me.

On the outskirts of the parish to the south, Rookwood stood as it had for the past 600 years with a cluster of cottages around it. Nearer the village was Bittles or Abbey Farm, and at the bottom of Well Hill where the road from Fareham and Southwick joined the Portsmouth road there was a farmhouse, now called Hook Vinney. Here in 1800 Mr. Thomas Butler had just installed the Hambledon Hunt's first pack of hounds.

Early in the year Mr. Butler had agreed to collect a pack of foxhounds of between twenty and thirty couples, to kennel them (which he did at Hook Vinney) and to maintain them. Members paid an annual subscription of ten guineas. It was agreed that the hounds should go out at least five times a fortnight and that no weather should stop them unless the snow was one foot deep at the kennel door. In its early days the Hambledon Hunt wore green coats in the hunting field, but later reverted to the traditional pink. In 1978 the expanding hunt found itself short of country while, at about the same time, the Hursley Hunt found itself short of funds. A happy marriage took place and the Hursley Hambledon Hunt flourishes today, covering the land from Petersfield to Salisbury.

38 The main road from Portsmouth where it joins the minor road from Fareham (*c*.1908). The horses, which seem to have some military connection, are opposite the entrance to Poore's Farm.

39 Poore's Farm *c*.1915 was also known as Bury Lodge Farm and Lee's Farm. It is now a private house called Hook Vinney.

A quarter of a mile from Hook Vinney, towards the village, stood Bury Lodge, the old house where Thomas Symons had entertained Charles II in 1651. In 1800 it was bought by Thomas Butler, who found it in such bad condition that he had it pulled down and rebuilt further back from the road. Thomas Sueter, the former ladies' man and Hambledon wicket-keeper and now a much respected member of the Hambledon choir, assisted in this work which was completed in 1808. The farm cottage adjoining the old Bury Lodge—the actual house in which Charles is thought to have slept—had been leased to the Brew family and was, in 1800, known as Brew's Bake House.

The next house towards the village was the cottage known today as 'Snowdrop Cottage'. Here in the early 1800s Robert Littlefield brought his bride Mary. Soon after they settled into this cottage they planted their initials 'M.R.L.' with snowdrops in their small front garden. From the bulbs of this sentimental gesture are descended the mass of snowdrops which gave the cottage its name and still delight Hambledonians each February nearly two centuries later.

Hambledon was well supplied with inns at this time. The old flint road, which was often awash in winter, first passed the *Green Man*, where Green Lane turned off towards the Meon Valley. Peter Stewart, another of the Hambledon cricketers—the suave comedian nicknamed 'Buck'—had once been landlord here, but he had died in 1796 and the pub was now in other hands. Then came the *Vine* and, less than a hundred yards away, the *Bell Inn*. Opposite the *Vine* was the Hambledon Brewery owned by D. Lunn & Co., which extended from the present Orchard House to Vernon House. Then nearer the heart of the village, almost opposite the 600-year-old Manor Farm, was the *New Inn*, the scene of the ill-fated meeting between James Stares and John Taylor which led to brutal murder and its consequent grim retribution. Behind this inn stood the large, rambling vicarage with its false William and Mary front which had replaced the Georgian front that had at some time been added to the Tudor core of the house. In 1800 William Stevens had been vicar of Hambledon for some 44 years and was now approaching the end of his days.

In the early years of the 19th century visitors to the village, who now included one or two of the first cricket pilgrims like Mr. Weir, could not fail to notice the air of shabbiness that pervaded, and which was especially obvious in the village centre. The great tithe barn belonging to the Manor Farm had a neglected tumbledown appearance and the Market Hall was also in need of repair; indeed it was to fall down in 1819. The houses lining the west side of the High Street told the same story—they were thirsty for paint, their roofs pockmarked by broken or missing tiles, their thatch ravaged by sparrows or rats. Even the newer houses on the east side, rebuilt after the fire about seventy years previously, and which included another inn, the *Red Lion*, looked desolate and uncared for.

Above the High Street, behind its old yew tree, stood the church. Despite its newly rebuilt tower it had a shabby air; inside there was ample evidence of the need for restoration and repair. Even the *George Inn* at the bottom of the High Street, where, in the time of Richard Nyren's landlordship, the annual cricket dinners had been held, was no exception to the general air of decline and neglect.

Behind the *George* and its stables and coach houses was Hambledon House, and here there was a difference, for the wealthy were increasing their wealth while the poor were finding life harder and harder. The Hale family lived in this bright, clean Georgian house standing in its well-kept garden. For seven years previous to 1800 Edward Hale had kept a pack of harriers at Hambledon House. When he died in 1823 this pack was taken over by Thomas Butler and hunted by him until 1834, after which time they were taken over by the Higgens family of Fairfield House.

Mr. Land lived at Park House until his death in 1791. He had kept a pack of foxhounds with which he hunted deer in the summer and fox in the winter in the Forest of Bere and around Hambledon. A contemporary writer, quoted in *Sporting Reminiscences of Hampshire*, remarked with astonishment how these hounds on the scent of a cub in the autumn would pass through deer they had hunted all summer. It is not known what happened to this pack after Mr. Land's death, but his huntsman, Will James, became huntsman to the Hambledon Hunt under Thomas Butler in 1800.

Between Broadhalfpenny and Chidden stood The Hermitage. No one knows how old the oldest parts of this are. It is said that a hermit or recluse used to live in this house, but there is no evidence of this. In 1800 the 58-year-old bachelor Admiral Sir Erasmus Gower lived there. He went to sea at a very early age as a captain's servant and first circumnavigated the globe as an Able Seaman. Promoted to Lieutenant on his return, he almost immediately sailed round the world again in the 30-year-old *Swallow*— a hazardous, adventure-packed voyage taking three years. Between 1770 and 1779 he served in several ships, being shipwrecked once and seeing plenty of action.

In 1779 the Commander-in-Chief West Indies Station, Sir George Rodney, asked for Mr. Gower to be appointed First Lieutenant of his flagship, H.M.S. *Sandwich*. In a spectacular action the following year 26 Spanish ships were captured, including the 64-gun ship-of-the-line *Guisuscoana*. She was commissioned as a British ship-of-the-line by Sir George, renamed *Prince William* and Mr. Gower was appointed in command. The Admiralty took the unusual step of confirming this appointment, so that Captain Gower now commanded a ship-of-the-line and escaped passing through the intermediate rank of Commander of a sloop-of-war.

In 1798 the neglect of service conditions and maintenance of the fleet had reached a hitherto unsurpassed nadir, and in consequence there came a day when the ships at Spithead refused to put to sea. The mutiny spread to the *Nore*, and for some weeks London was virtually under blockade by the British fleet. Commodore Sir Erasmus Gower was sent to Chatham to deal with this situation, and he appears to have done so successfully and fairly, for shortly afterwards these same ships fired a royal salute in honour of the Sovereign's birthday with such gusto that part of the rotting fortifications of Sheerness tumbled down. His highest honour was his last job. In 1804 he was appointed Commander-in-Chief and Governor of Newfoundland, where his humane disposition and wisdom made a great impact during his three years of office. He returned to The Hermitage in 1807, and in 1810 the young Able Seaman, who had sailed round the world with Commodore Byron, received his last honour; he was promoted Admiral of the White.

Sir Erasmus had clearly been a man of great courage at sea, but on land he is said to have lived in dread of falling trees, bricks or tiles. On windy nights at The Hermitage he would often go out and walk about on the open Holt. He died in his home in 1814.

North-west of The Hermitage lay Chidden, and west of Chidden was West End, the home, in 1800, of John Goldsmith and his wife Elizabeth (my great-great-great-grandparents). John Goldsmith, who was one of the churchwardens, had lived a full life which was now drawing to a close. He and his son, John, had both played cricket during the Hambledon Cricket Club's golden days, but neither of them laid any claim to stardom, nor did they play in any of the 'Great Matches'.

Sad as the state of the church may have seemed, sad as the derelict tithe barn and market hall appeared, sad as was the rate at which small houses became dirty hovels, the saddest of all the places where the shadow of neglect and poverty had fallen was the *Bat and Ball Inn*. Deserted, desolate and neglected, it had now scarcely more company than the sheep which grazed on the immortal plot before it.

In 1803 Britain was the only obstacle in the way of Napoleon's grandiose designs, and in May began the most desperate conflict in which this country had ever been engaged. The French invasion force, the magnificent 'Army of England'—100,000 strong—was assembled in northern France with 2,000 flat-bottomed boats to ferry it across the Channel. In fact the 'Army of England' never left the continent but, as the threat of invasion was very real, the 'Volunteer Corps for the Defence of the Realm' was formed.

Hampshire's quota was 5,000 men. Within a few days of the call 20,000 from the county had volunteered. The Hambledon Volunteers, previously formed in 1779 and disbanded two years later as an earlier threat of war receded, formed once more and stood by to repel the invader like the Home Guard which was to succeed it 136 years later. By Royal Commission dated 21 February 1800 Thomas Martin Palmer was appointed Lieutenant Colonel Commandant of the Hambledon and Wickham Volunteers, but 'not to take rank in Our Army except during the time of the said Corps being called out into actual Service ...'

Thomas Palmer's daughters, Millicent and Anna, wove and presented the Hambledon Volunteers with their colours. For many years these flags were carried in procession on heydays and highdays, until they were finally laid up in the church. They hang now in the south aisle, nearly two hundred years old, so frail and worn that it is scarcely possible to make out the letters, which are 'H V' with the simple motto *Pro Rege et Patria*—For King and Country. The Corps was finally disbanded in 1810.

In 1815 Napoleon was sent as a captive to Saint Helena, surrounded by the restless seas that had always baffled him, and in England, superficially at any rate, there was wealth and splendour untold. But beneath the surface a very different state of affairs existed. A great majority of the people were sunk in squalid poverty, while the population was increasing by leaps and bounds. Children of eight years old were in many cases working 14 hours a day to earn a few pence, and vast numbers had no work and no pence at all.

The population of England in 1811 was 10,000,000 people; by 1851 it had risen to 18,000,000. Although the great landowners had improved their methods of food production, they could not keep pace with the demands of the increasing population in near starvation conditions. In the rural areas great numbers left their villages to seek employment in the towns and cities, but there the machinery of the Industrial Revolution was putting more and more people out of work. Many merely left the appalling conditions in their villages for the revolting slums of the towns. The wild competition for employment kept wages desperately low, and the only remedy for the misery in which so many were plunged was private charity or the Poor Law, through which grants were made in supplement of wages.

The great wealth which Britain was now earning was going into the pockets of a small rich class, and there was a vast gulf fixed between the rich and the labouring mass. The widely diffused comfort which had been a feature of 'Merrie England' had vanished. William Cobbett, that vivid journalist, shrewd observer and lover of the country and country people, wrote that the well-fed peasantry he had known in his youth had been replaced by 'a population of starvelings living in hovels and feeding on slops and tea'. George III was nominally king of England at this time but, by 1800, he was afflicted by porphyria which was causing intermittent bouts of madness, and his son, the Regent, was a dissolute fop.

It is possible that Hambledon weathered these hard times better than many other places. The memory of the all-embracing Broadhalfpenny spirit must still have lingered, while the humane efforts of the vicars and other families who lived in the larger houses and cared about the village and its less fortunate people did much to relieve distress. In 1820 the vicar, the Rev. Richard Richards, bought a house in East Street and almost certainly installed several families. In 1824 William Higgens of Fairfield, John Goldsmith of West End and John Foster of Park, following the vicar's example, acquired twenty properties in the village and let them out at an affordable rate similar to the Housing Associations of today.* Nevertheless hard times there were; the price of bread was beyond the reach of many families, and the call of nearby Portsmouth caused a decline in Hambledon that was swift and shattering.

William Cobbett visited Hambledon in 1822 and 1826, staying on both occasions with my great-great-grandfather at West End. Cobbett was more attracted to the hills surrounding Hambledon than to the village itself, which did not impress him. The market hall had collapsed and the fairs amounted to little more than two or three gingerbread stalls with dolls and whistles for children. The church, like the village, 'was a tumbledown rubbishy place'. Cobbett blamed Hambledon's state on 'that hellish assemblage' Portsmouth, Gosport and Portsea, for which so many countrymen left their native villages in the hope of finding life less cruel, so often only to find conditions even worse.

It was about the time of Cobbett's visits to Hambledon that a house that was to bear our village's name was built close to the notorious John Macarthur's Elizabeth

---

* Such as Lashly Meadow, mentioned in the next chapter.

Farm in New South Wales, Australia. Today the Parramatta and District Historical Society of New South Wales has its office and headquarters at 'Hambledon', Hassall Street, Parramatta.

In the early years of the century, John Macarthur, founder of the Australia Wool Industry, and his wife Elizabeth sent their eldest daughter, also Elizabeth, to England to complete her education, but she was too delicate to withstand 'the harsh English climate'. In 1805 she returned to Sydney on the *Argo* with her father and Miss Penelope Lucas of Hambledon and some Merino sheep from Windsor. Penelope was originally engaged as governess to the three Macarthur daughters, but became a lifelong friend and companion to Mrs. Elizabeth Macarthur. It seems that in 1805 Miss Lucas was 'a little ancient for a Miss' (she was 37) and so assumed the title of 'Mrs.'. Twenty-two years later, in March 1827, Mrs. Lucas moved into the cottage and named it Hambledon, and there she died in 1836 aged sixty-eight.

Today Hambledon Cottage (so called although it is fairly spacious) is considered one of the foremost of Australian historical places; it is certainly one of the oldest cottages still standing. For years it became a holiday home for Governors, and in its early days within the domain of the Macarthurs it must have seen stirring times and characters.

Back in England, in 1830, the industrial discontent in the growing towns and cities drove both businessmen and their workers into political action. There was an epidemic of strikes in the north, and some talk of a march on London. In the southern counties from Kent to Wiltshire the poverty in the villages and farms led to a sort of peasants' revolt in the summer, which was later called the 'Swing Riots'. Many of the gentry were behind the peasants, and in Hambledon a General Gough was an active leader. During the disturbances landlords received threatening letters signed 'Captain Swing', and hundreds of ricks were burnt. Turmoil, upheaval and full revolution seemed imminent. Instead there was a General Election.

The birth of the reforms that were to follow was a difficult one, and the child, when it arrived, was a mean, meagre little fellow. The first reform, the Factory Act of 1833, prohibited the use of children under nine in the cotton factories and limited the hours that older children might work to nine a day! By 1843 the improved conditions in town and country (though still horrifying by our 20th-century standards) had stilled the ugly cries for reform, and matters continued to improve. The repeal of the hated import tax on foreign corn finally reduced the price of bread. Slowly wages rose and the cost of living decreased.

In Hambledon the bitter period culminating in the Swing Riots of 1830 gave way to one of hope and of not such absolute grinding poverty. Nonetheless, the population of the village continued to increase. By 1831 it had risen to 2,026 souls, and in March 1834 'The Vestry'—the assembled churchwardens and others who ran village affairs— met and resolved to encourage destitute but able-bodied young men to emigrate to the British Settlements in Canada. They agreed to furnish any volunteers with the necessary outfit, pay their passage and allow them 'such necessary aid as may be deemed sufficient on their landing in Canada'. All this was reckoned to amount to about £15 per head.

40   The Poor House in East Street, *c*.1907. It is now a private residence.

This may seem a generous gesture, and indeed it was when you consider the purchasing power of £15 one hundred and seventy years ago, the equivalent of—very roughly—£700 today. The Vestry had, though, calculated that the cost to the Parish of maintaining these paupers, 'in the course of a very few years ... will equal the rental of all the lands and tenements as at present assessed'.

In 1850 there began a period of actual contentment, difficult to understand today, borne on the wings of future hope and promise, nourished by the strength of the family unit and the compassion of the whole parish community and warmed by the glow of Britain's growing imperial greatness. Nevertheless, by the end of the century, neighbouring Portsmouth was still an ugly, unhealthy place containing revolting slums, while in Hambledon the majority of people were still sunk in ignorance, with hours of work far too long and conditions of labour often cruelly hard. The mass of working people had no protection against distress due to sickness or unemployment except private charity and the harsh assistance of the Poor Law. A visitor to the village in 1900 would not see such desolation as his predecessor of a hundred years earlier, but he would still see the stirring of social unrest which, like the years before 1830, could have erupted in open rebellion but for another General Election—this time the astonishing General Election of 1906. But these events have their place in the next century and in the next chapter.

Mr. W.H. Barkworth of Cams was a man of considerable means, and a very keen sportsman, playing cricket and hunting regularly with the Hambledon Hunt. In December 1834 he had a lucky escape when hunting on Fisher's Farm land near Basing Park. His horse fell into a pit excavated for building stone but concealed by weeds and brushwood.

The horse was killed and William Barkworth only avoided the same fate by being thrown clear, over the horse's head. His son, John Boulderson Barkworth, was a devoted churchman who did much for the church. He put in a turret staircase for the belfry, the west door in the tower and paid half the cost of a new buttress at the north-west angle. He had a new frame made for the bells, had one recast, provided the church clock, presented a silver service for use at Communion and inserted several stained-glass windows. He also presented a pair of fine silver candlesticks. However, from the 1930s onwards, they were not used because they did not match the brass altar cross. For years they lay unseen and untouched in a drawer in the vestry until, in 1960, they were presented to the new church at Borrowdale near Salisbury, Rhodesia (as Zimbabwe was then called), where my brother, David, was the organist. He, like Penelope Lucas in Australia, also called his house 'Hambledon'.

Towards the end of the 19th century, a time drawn so darkly by historians, there emerged two pictures of Hambledon full of sunshine and happiness. They were penned by two women in very different circumstances but who had one thing in common— their love for Hambledon. One, a young girl in service, kept a journal; the other, widowed within a year of her marriage, wrote a small, delightful book.

John Ventham lived and worked as a labourer at Whitedale Farm. On 7 July 1870, his youngest daughter, Mary Laura, was born and in due course she attended Hambledon School, founded in 1848. In 1886, at the age of 15, Mary went into service at Court House in the village, and two years later she began her journal.

Today we are apt to look back in horror, anger even, at the idea of young girls in service, 'trapped, enslaved'. Such was not always the case, as the following extracts taken from Mary's diary indicate. Life was less complex in those days; joys and sorrows were simply expressed over simple matters by people less sophisticated than their descendants today. Mary was a deeply religious girl, and her journal is spattered with religious texts. ('I must try and put down a little of the sermon that was preached ...') The writing is fine, beautifully clear, though almost entirely bereft of punctuation. There are a few spelling mistakes and the occasional grammatical slip as may be seen. I have added some punctuation marks for the sake of clarity.

January Sunday 15th 1888

The new year has come again and it has brought to me a new idea to write a little of my daily life. I have now been in service nearly two year. I am living in a Gentlemans house where there are three servants kept—a cook, parlour maid and myself i am housemaid. I am very happy, even happier than I was at my own home for I have more to occupy my mind although there are many little troubles and vexations to go through but we must not expect it to be all smooth. the Cook is a kind Mothery person. She often tries to correct me when I am not doing things as it should be done, but I only answer her angrily. But I have learnt a lesson today, our Curate preached a sermon about being obedient to those who are over us and not to answer back, so I will try and not do it again ... Jane [the parlourmaid] is a year or two older than me. She is full of life and fun, we get on fairly well together and are all happy. There are six in the family when they are all home very kind people. I was confirmed when I was fifteen ...

January Sunday 15. 1888

The new year has come again and it has brought to me a new idea to write a little of my daily life I have now been in service nearly two year I am living in a gentlemas house where there are three servants kept that Cook parlourmaid and myself i am housemaid I am very happy even happier than I was at my own home for I have more to occupy my mind although there are many little troubles and vexation to go through but we must not expect it to be all smooth. the Cook is a kind Mothery person she often tries to correct me when I am not doing things as it should be done but I only answer her angrily but I have learnt

41 The first page of Mary Ventham's journal.

My home is only about a quarter of an hours walk from where I am living. It is a sweet pretty place, trees and hills all round it. My father is a farm labourer. He looks after the farm and the sheep, wich is his great delight. My mother is a kind thoughtful woman. She looks after me in every way and sometimes I feel rather ungrateful. I have four sisters and one brother ... my eldest sister is married and living in London and have got three little girls. My other sisters are in service and my brother is in the police force at Lymington ... I goes home every week and I looks forward to it with pleasure for I loves my home and all who are there ... There is one pet in my present home that is a dog his name is rover. He is a kind faithful friend.

Monday February 16th 1888.

I woke up so happy. It was a beautiful day. I went for the butter. There was a funeral, I met my sister in the churchyard, she asked me to go into the church. Something told me not to go, but the temptation was so great. I went in and of course I had the dog. I thought he would be alright outside, but as soon as I got inside, he came in, and I had a great bother with him. I was very sorry indeed, so I went for my walk with a very heavy heart to think I had given way to sin.

There were no entries between March and November 1888. It had been a sad and busy summer. On November 14th Mary records '... We have lost our dear Mistress. She was ill only a few days. I loved her so much ... I felt I had lost a real friend.'

42 Mary Ventham aged about twenty.

This 14th November was Emma, the cook's, 32nd birthday and impetuous Mary decides to dash out and get some figs and sweets. 'I was so happy and in such a hurry to get away that taking my hat off the dresser, I pulled off a dish cover and broke it all to pieces, so again I went out with a heavy heart.'

Throughout 1889 Mary wrote little about the daily routine of her work. Her entries chiefly described her walks in the countryside with her sisters and 'dear old rover'.

In May 1889 she wrote:

> Went out in the afternoon through the fields up into the wood and I do not think I had ever seen a prettier sight. We sat upon a style at the top of the hill and looked down into the village nothing scarcely moving but the trees of all kinds laden with their splendid blossom, the fields waving their crops of corn so green and the meadows strewed with yellow and white and the bells were ringing for service. At the distance we could hear the chapel people singing and preaching [the Ebenezer Chapel was built in 1865] and then we passed on through the woods. It was lovely, the woods were so nice and shady but I must not dwell to long upon this. I must look back to see what we have been doing. We have been very busy lately house cleaning, we have almost finished now. My sister have been down to help us and I am pleased for she gets on so nicely ...

43 Hambledon, *c.*1907, as Mary Ventham would have seen it from 'a style *(sic)* at the top of the hill'.

Sunday June 15th [1890]

There seems to be a lot come and gone again last Sunday. My sister from Emsworth
was home and her young man And my brother with his young woman was home and
I went home for the afternoon and Evening. My eldest sister was home with all her
children, so we were all home but one sister, fifteen of us to tea. It was a happy
gathering ... Today I have been for a walk with my sister up to a farm called Glidden,
but it is nothing but ruins now for nearly all the building was pulled down by people
from far and near and the other night the remains caught fire and it is almost all burnt
down. It was the home of two ladies I knew very well. Once I remember going there
when I was gleaning and they gave me milk, and once I went there to tea, with the Band
of Hope children, as one of our young ladies is the head of the Band of Hope. I used
to belong to it, but somehow one day when I was helping Mother tie corn, I drank some
beer, so I came out of it, but I am in the Temperance Society now ... There was a great
many people up there [at Glidden]. One young man I saw from the village up there.
I spoke to him and he caught us up coming back and walked a short distance with us.
He gave me his white pinks he had in his coat. He is a very nice young man. I think
I may say he rather waits for me, but of course I must not go for walks with him, for
Mother would not like it if she knew it. I would not like to do what she did not like
me to, but there what am I writing? Young girls are fanciful sometimes. I was this
morning when a Great rat bounded from the cellar stairs close to my feet. I screamed,
raced up the stairs, told the girls a rat was coming upstairs after me ... I was so
frightened I couldend stop to walk up stairs. I came up and I felt ready to faint. Of
course I made a great commotion, but they had out dear old rover from his masters
room and with brooms and all the rest they found it and rover bounding up the passage
after it, knocked down Miss Lydia [and] killed the rat. What a set out it was.

January 11th 1891.

... I have been to church this morning and out with Emma [the cook] and my sister this afternoon. We went round Rushmoor to see the skaters. There was a lot up there, it is a shame to spend the Sabboth that way ... It is a dreadful hard winter. You can hardly stand on the roads, they are so slippery. I have fallen down five times.

July 5th [1891].

Sunday again, and the last Sunday Jane [the parlourmaid] and me will spend together, for she is going away and i am to take her place and her youngest sister is coming to take my place. I hope we shall get on all right. I mean to try hard, as it will be better for me, and i am getting so old, i shall be 21 years next Tuesday. I shan't have quite so much time to go out with the dogs to ramble in the hayfields where they are all at work, my own dear Father labouring on as if nothing ever put him out and always his loving smile for me. How beautiful is a fathers love. It cheers my heart to feel my hands clasped in his and his lips upon my cheek as if I was yet a infant. I am writing this so as the years go on I may like to feel the happiness that i feel now.

On Palm Sunday 1892 Mary again enthuses about the beauty of spring and adds rather wistfully, '... the young man I wrote of [with the white pinks] still walks with us sometimes. He is very good not to get tired of me. My Mother likes him better now. He gave me a few primroses to day. I like him but I dont think he will ever be my young man.'

44   Mary Ventham and Annie Wright outside their teashop, *c*.1920.

The journal of this happy, impulsive, innocent, deeply religious girl who loved her home, her large extended family, her village and those she worked for and with, shines like a dapple of sunlight in the gloom of late 19th-century England. She would have been a wonderful mother and grandmother but this was not to be. Mary never married her beau with the white pinks or anybody else. In later years she lived in Porchester where she ran a sweetshop with Annie Wright, who had been in service with her. She died in 1950 aged 80.

Nowhere in Mary's journal was there any mention of sickness except for the short illness and death of her beloved mistress in 1888. Nevertheless diseases did sweep through the village from time to time, with devastating results. It was when scarlet fever, measles, whooping cough and 'the sore throat' visited the village that Father Time unshipped his scythe from his shoulder, as he had done over the pre-penicillin years of earlier centuries. At these times the parish registers list the names of adults and children alike who 'died of a sore throat'. By 1883 'the sore throat' had a name—diphtheria.

The school log for that year tells us that during the week ending 6 July the attendance considerably decreased as most of the older children were involved in getting the hay in—'haying'. The following week the attendance was again depleted as the children were still 'haying'. On the Tuesday afternoon the school was closed for the Band of Hope tea party at Glidden. During the week ending 20 July several cases of illness were reported. One day during the next week nine-year-old William Gough of Beccles was taken ill and sent home. On Saturday 28 July William died and several other cases of diphtheria followed. Young Alfred Reed was taken ill on 31 July and the village lived in fear and horror as the deaths mounted. On 4 August the School Board met with Mr. Clough, a surgeon, and the Hambledon physician, Dr. Earl, acting for the local Sanitary Authority. The meeting lasted six hours and resulted in the board agreeing to close the school and giving the necessary permission for it to be used as a temporary hospital. The school remained closed for 14 weeks, and on 5 November the Log lists the names of eight boys (including William Gough's brother, George) who died in that period. Under this list there is a heading 'In the Infant Department'; a space was left but no names were entered. Finally there is another list of 19 boys and girls under the heading—'Names of children from families who have suffered from diphtheria excluded from attendance at school by Sanitary Order'.

Attendance remained low throughout November as parents objected to sending their children back so soon after the epidemic, and with good reason, for four more cases occurred. Even in the following term, in January 1884, the disease struck again. Penny Oakshot from Cams Lane survived it but two Batts children from Church Lane did not, and many children were kept at home for fear of infection. The tide of deaths ceased on 11 January 1884 with that of little Nellie Batts. She was the fifteenth child to be buried. During this terrible period from June 1883 to January 1884, 22 households containing 132 inhabitants had been touched by the epidemic; 80 managed to survive. Needless to say the school premises were thoroughly inspected by Dr. Parsons, of the Local Government Board, and Dr. Earl. The well water was tested and 'found to be good'.

45   Hambledon School, 1994.

Seventeen or eighteen years before this epidemic, in 1866, many Hambledonians might have noticed Dora Higgens of Fairfield House in various parts of the parish, sitting on her stool with her sketching pad on her knees. They would have guessed that she was making these sketches to remind her, in the years to come, of the village that had been her home for the past 27 years, and which she was shortly to leave. The whole village knew of her engagement to William Goldsmith, formerly of West End, who had just gone to Australia, where he was making ready their new home in Towoomba. She would be missed by many, for she was much loved and respected.

In the summer of 1867 she left Hambledon as she thought for ever, and married William in Queensland. Early one morning, rather less than year after their wedding, William woke, tormented by earache. All the home remedies were applied, for there was no proper medical aid within hundreds of miles of the new family homestead in Towoomba, but the pain grew worse as the abscess in his ear took firmer hold and its deadly poison spread. By the time a doctor arrived it was too late; William was dead. In 1868 Dora Goldsmith returned to her old home. As time passed, her misery and pain yielded to the affection and sympathies of her many friends and her own love of Hambledon.

She had many childhood memories. One in particular was the time when she was about six years old and had gone off on her own in search of some wild flowers. Climbing over the northern boundary fence of Fairfield's grounds, she had fallen into a bed of nettles by the path that led below the field where the village school was shortly to be built. Stung and sore she sat on the footpath crying, when old General Gough came walking by with his stick.

'Hello,' he said, 'and what are you crying about?'

'I don't know,' said little Dora.

The old man held out his hand. 'Come along then, I'll walk you back home. Will you come?' There was something so warm and friendly in the last three words that Dora took his hand and trotted back to Fairfield beside him. She wrote of him some sixty years later, mentioning that he was one of the leaders of the Swing Riots. 'I remember him as a kindly old man, always wearing a smock frock which kind of coat is rarely to be met with now.'

In church she always sat in the Higgens family pew which was in the south aisle. In the days of her childhood part of the Christmas decorations consisted of small sprigs of holly stuck in gimlet holes along the top of the pews. It always used to upset her that the branches with the most berries were reserved for the centre pews, while in the side aisles the berries 'were much wanting'.

Not only did she know all the villagers, but she also knew the gypsies, who often settled for a while around Hyden Wood. She occasionally went up to London. After her return from one such journey in her later years, she was telling one of her village friends how kind the London police were to her and all those who wanted help in crossing the street.

46 Dora Goldsmith, in 1898 aged 59, when she was living with her sister, Mary Higgens, at Glidden Farm. By this time the ruins of the earlier farmhouse had been removed and the land ploughed over.

'Ah, but they knows all about 'e up there!' came the reply. As Dora later remarked—
a doubtful compliment.

Dora Goldsmith, like John Nyren a century before her, spent the last years of her
life in Bromley, Kent, although she certainly made frequent visits to her beloved
Hambledon. In 1908 at the age of 69 she sat at her writing table and, although her room
may have overlooked the fields of Kent, she saw only the meadows, the distant woods
and houses of her home village. Scattered around her were sheaves of notes and the pen-
and-ink sketches of Hambledon she had made over forty years earlier to take with her to
Australia; before her lay a plain sheet of paper. She picked up her pen and began to write:

HAMBLEDON HANTS

Past and Present

Nestling in a valley of the south downs—beech woods clinging to the slopes of the
near hills (these woods known by the provincial name of 'hangers') lies the Village
of Hambledon.

The woods are carpeted in Spring with wood anemones (wind flowers), bluebells,
woodruff, looking like cut ivory, and in one spot is a patch of the rare plant Herb Paris.

The Village, not much known in the great world, feels itself this year of importance,
for the Centenary of Cricket is to be kept there on the old Broadhalfpenny Ground
near the *Bat and Ball Inn*, which was built when those first cricket matches were
played. [The occasion was the unveiling, on Broadhalfpenny Down on 10 September
1908, of the stone memorial to those earlier heroes of cricket. A match was also
arranged in which a Hambledon eleven, which included C.B. Fry, beat an All England
eleven by five wickets. The *Bat and Ball Inn*, originally known as *The Hut*, is much
older than Dora states.]

Then follows a passage about the Cricket Club, after which Dora Goldsmith's
book continues:

The Village, in bygone years, had its fair or market, and a hunt ball was held in the
George Inn, situated five miles from the high coach road running between London
and Portsmouth. *The Rocket*, and its driver, Faulkner, were well known. The writer
remembers as a very little girl, going by coach to London and seeing the horses
changed at one of the posting inns. The roads and lanes [about Hambledon] were very
flinty. Some friends coming from London with their carriage, coachman and horses,
found it a new experience, and not a good one.

To the north-west of Hambledon is Old Winchester Hill, crowned by its Roman
Encampment. The entrance to the encampment can be clearly traced and a moat
around it. [In fact it is an Iron Age hill fort probably dating from around the fifth
century B.C. and the 'moat' was a bare earth ditch.]

On the summit are three mounds. It is not known what they were for, nothing was
found on opening them. Old Winchester Hill overlooks the valley of the Meon, up
which the Jutes made their way from Southampton Water, and below is the very
ancient little Saxon church of Corhampton.

There are several roads leading out of the valley-village of Hambledon. In a field to
the left of the Fareham road, as you enter the valley, are the ancient British Barrows,

and not far away is an old farm house The Abbey Farm and, I have heard, in the thickness of its walls is a seeming priest's chamber. The Portsmouth and Fareham roads meet at the commencement of the Village. From the Springs in this area I have seen water flowing down the Village street, breaking up into clear little rills on the flinty road leading to Broadhalfpenny and flooding the floors of cottages and the cellars of the larger houses. Now the country is better drained, there is often a want of water in Hambledon, and the wells get very low.

Until a few years ago Hambledon was eight miles from the Rail, but now considers itself much in the world, for there is a station at Droxford, within four miles. Houses are springing up in Green Lane which is the road you follow to get to Droxford, and one of my old country friends calls this the 'West End' of Hambledon.

The Village streets are straggling and primitive. The corner shop, at the bottom of the High Street, was, in my young days, kept by Mr. Aburrow. His father was one of the noted cricketers. At the bottom of the High Street, in the middle of the Village, the determined Hambledonians lit the bonfire on Guy Fawkes day, and it was no easy matter to persuade them it was safer to have it elsewhere.

The church overlooks the Village. All of it, with the exception of the tower which was burnt down in 1788, being of an early date, partly Saxon, Norman and Early English. We are very proud of our church with its fine, simple arches and oaken roof. The chalk in the arches was said to have been dug out of Broadhalfpenny Down. The church was beautifully restored—not spoiled—about 30 or 40 years ago. The old high pews and reading desk, under which the clerk sat and responded for most of the congregation, were, as well as the galleries, cleared away. [This was in 1876, when more than £2,000 was spent on the fabric and fittings—the chancel was separately restored by the Ecclesiastical Commissioners. One sad fact not mentioned by Dora Goldsmith was that the old font which had been in the church for 400 years was removed and replaced by a new one as a memorial to Thomas Patterson, who had been vicar of Hambledon for 33 years, when he died in 1847. In 1880 the old font was given to Denmead parish church, where it is still in use today.]

Before my day there was an orchestral accompaniment of various instruments. I can well remember one of the old veteran singers giving a bass solo at Christmas. There is a splendid yew tree on the southern side of the church, protected by a railing kindly given. It has flourished grandly since thus protected, though the trunk is only a shell.

With all the changes there is something to be regretted. The white owl no longer makes its home in the church roof, from where it took its evening flights around; and, perhaps not to be regretted, was the removal of the bees which made their hive in the chancel roof, and whose wandering members agitated the congregation by settling in their bonnets or on their heads.

The National schools were built [behind the church to the north-east] in 1848. Before that day there was a Dame's school. Dame Parret, I think was the name, and Mr. Thumbwood had a school in the High Street for the boys.

If you keep to the North Road, in time you will reach Broadhalfpenny Down. The street goes straggling on, here and there a few yards of twist-ankle pavement, all of which is characteristic. Further on is the path under Whitedale wall, a kind of Village promenade in the early days of white petticoats. In that country of muddy lanes it was a cause of thankfulness when petticoats of brushing material were introduced, though the first scarlet ones were looked upon as 'hardly the thing'!

A great improvement for Hambledon was the planting of trees on Windmill Down [about 1880] which was the Village cricket ground. A lover of wild flowers would rejoice in Hambledon, but I fear many of their haunts are cleared away. In the hedgerows and banks, in March and April one gathered dark purple, dull pink and white violets. The fly, bee, twyblade, man, lady's tress, birds nest and sweet butterfly orchis were to be found as well as the more common early purple and spotted orchis. The copses were a delight to the eye, spangled with primroses, bluebells and graceful little white anemones. What a prize it was to find an oxslip! Later in the summer there were quantities of wild strawberries growing in the copses. At Rudley Mill, in the parish, one paddled in the water to gather the bog bean, with its feathery blossom. In the early winter the hedges are draped with old man's beard (wild clematis). Rather a rarity were the brilliant red cup fungi, which grew on old bits of wood in hedges and banks. There was a great freedom allowed to wander in and around the Village. Boards, 'Trespassers will be prosecuted', so noticeable in many districts, were happily very little in evidence.

The Village gaieties were the Club Feasts and the Bower Dance. This last was the Hambledon fête especially, and in the Jubilee year it was revived. [1897—Queen Victoria's Diamond Jubilee.] The Ball-room—a framework covered with green branches inside and out, and decorated with flowers—was erected in a field, [perhaps where the house 'Bower Mead' now stands] and in it the dancing went on. Some of the old folk were splendid at country dances. The Mummers came at Christmas time. Their songs and acting were a survival of the old miracle plays. There was the Village Band—the beating of the drum being a strong point in the music—and the Handbell Ringers also came and gave us some of the old tunes. *The British Grenadiers* was a favourite with the Band.

On the Club Days, in the summer, a procession of the members headed by the band and flag bearers, marched to the different houses. The flags were presented to the Volunteers by Millicent Palmer and her sister by whom they were made. Their father commanded the Volunteers when 'Bony' might be expected at any moment to invade the coast, and the trained bands be called out.

Hambledon is within twelve miles of Portsmouth, and in the days of the Press Gang [up to 1815] only one man went with a team into the town. The horses could not return alone, but if two men went with the wagon, one might be pressed.

Hambledon lads, from time to time, have come to the front. Lashley, who was one of Captain Scott's men aboard *The Discovery* claims the village as his birthplace. [More of Lashly—his name is properly spelt without the 'e'—in the next chapter.]

Glidden Farm lies above Broadhalfpenny Down. The dear old house and its surroundings no longer exist. The whole property, owing to a protracted lawsuit, became for some years no man's land—a camping place for disorder and destruction. The old farm house was pulled down bit by bit, the outbuildings wrecked, the timber cut down and the land left uncultivated, the cottages burned, the whole place left desolate. In the time before the Civil Wars it had belonged to the family of Glidden, who in those troublous days left their native land for America. I believe there are now descendents of the name of Glidden in Boston, U.S. America. Some of the family twice visited the home of their ancestors, and it was a pleasure to give them a sketch of the old house. [The family still visit the site of their old home. Their present address is in Newcastle, Lincoln Co., Maine.]

Another remembrance of the Village is the truffle hunter. For miles he used to walk with his little dogs to dig out the rare delicacies which his dogs scented at the foot of beech trees. The truffle dogs were covered in short curls like lambs.

At Garnet's Farm kegs of brandy and smuggled goods were kept in a chamber down a large well. A bucket was let down with a man in it, who caught a hook placed in the wall, drew himself to the side and so got into the store.

Before my day, living in the Village was a Mr. Garnet. He had been in the Commissariat at the time of the Peninsular War. There was delay in finding food for the troops. Sir Thomas Picton said, 'If my soldiers don't have food before tomorrow morning, I will hang you, Garnet, on that tree.' Mr. Garnet referred the matter to Sir Arthur Wellesley, afterwards the Duke of Wellington, who answered, 'Did Picton say that? Then be sure, Garnet, he will do it.' The food was forthcoming.

I still love my native village where, after an absence of years, I always receive a warm welcome. This must be my excuse for writing this little account of the Hampshire village of Hambledon.

I hope its Cricket Club may flourish. May the young men and maidens grow up good, and be an honour to their village. Perhaps in the future, Hambledon may have its local Museum, Musical Society, Band and Flower Show, and develop healthy interests and fun for its young people, who, though they may go out into the larger world, will still have a true pride and clinging feeling to their old home, Hambledon, and worthily maintain its old reputation.

DORA GOLDSMITH

***

On 7 October in the following year, 1909, Dora died and was buried at Bromley. On the south wall of the chancel of Hambledon church there is a bronze and enamel plaque in memory of her husband, William, who died in Towoomba at the age of twenty-nine. Beneath this there is a rather attractive brass plate which bears the following words:

In loving memory of
DORA GOLDSMITH
- Wife of -
William Gale Goldsmith and daughter of W.J.J. Higgens
all of Hambledon.
This brass is placed by relations & friends
who loved her.
Departed this life Oct. 7th 1909. Aged 70 years.
'To live in hearts we leave behind, is not to die.'

The School in 1866 from Fairfield Walk

Chapter 13

Living Memory

Three times in its long history Hambledon, in company with the southern counties, had been on the brink of revolt—once in the 14th century when the manor was ready to join Wat the Tyler and his embattled tillers of the soil, once during the Swing Riots of the 19th century and once again in this 20th century when rebellion was only just avoided by a flood of reforms and the more devastating disaster of the First World War of 1914.

In January 1901 Queen Victoria died, and the British people, with all the pomp and ceremony of those days, mourned the passing of 'The Great White Queen'.

After this long and, in many ways, great reign there was bound to be change. The rumblings of revolt, reverberating all too near the surface of brittle splendour that lay over the British way of life, seemed certain to erupt in 1906. Instead, as in 1830, there was a General Election, one of the most sensational this country had ever witnessed. The Conservative Party lost most of its leaders, the Liberals swept into power and 51 members of the new Labour Party took their seats in Westminster.

In the next four years reform followed reform. They included measures to protect children and old age pensioners; there were industrial reforms and tax reforms; the unwholesome, sordid conditions in cities were tackled and, in the country areas, a serious attempt was made to revive British agriculture and to stimulate hope among the peasantry. Today all these reforms appear archaic; even in their own time they were felt by many to be but a beginning, and a poor beginning at that. Life, though, was not all dark and oppressive. There was still some cricket and football, and the friendly companionship of a closely knit village where joys and hardships were shared. There were the races at Hambledon's racecourse near Stoke Wood. Hambledon Race Day was a school holiday and the children used to collect posies of bluebells, primroses and cowslips and would throw them up into the passing horse-drawn coaches, scrambling afterwards in the road for pennies from the racegoers. This tradition stopped after the tragic death of nine-year-old Dorothy Rowe, who was run over in Denmead. The

121

remains of the old grandstand can still be seen. It was built to replace a stand which collapsed in 1880 while it was supporting 300 people; many were injured but fortunately no one was killed. The Hambledon Hunt was also popular and there was a roller-skating rink in Green Lane near Coombe Down.

There was also a great interest in Captain Scott's two expeditions in the Antarctic, because in 1901 Leading Stoker William Lashly joined the *Discovery*. He was born and brought up in Hambledon and attended the village school. He was one of a family of three boys and two girls. In 1880, when he was 13, he worked for his father who was a thatcher, but in 1889 he joined the Royal Navy. In 1896 he married, and his daughter was born four years later.

From 1901, when the *Discovery* sailed from London, Lashly kept a diary. In this he records, with great modesty, how he managed to save both Captain Scott and Petty Officer Edgar Evans when they had fallen into a crevass. Other diarists on the expedition, and there was no shortage of them, commented on William Lashly's alertness, intelligent observation, his physical strength, tireless enthusiasm and utter dependability.

In 1910 Lashly, now Stoker Chief Petty Officer, joined the *Terra Nova* for Scott's last expedition. On 4 January 1912 when they were 156 miles from the South Pole, Captain Scott decided to make the last, ill-fated dash with Captain Oates, Dr. Wilson, Lieutenant Bowers and Petty Officer Edgar Evans. He ordered Lieutenant R.G.R. Evans to return to Base Camp with Lashly and Petty Officer Tom Crean.

Greatly disappointed, they commenced the 800-mile slog northwards, back to Hut Point Camp. Being summer in the south they had 24 hours of daylight and temperatures ranging from 10 degrees Fahrenheit to -25, blizzards, high winds, crevasses, glacial heights to descend and times of deep, soft snow as well as good conditions of hard flat areas—and a heavy sledge to haul. On 27 January Lashly recorded in his diary that he had been out 96 days. On 5 February he wrote, 'I am beginning to suspect something is wrong with Mr. Evans.' On the 10th—'I am sorry to say Mr. Evans is suffering from scurvy and very badly. Of course we knew this but we have to get along and not look on the bad side. But the time have come when we must take the greatest care of him.'

On 11 February Lashly and Crean built a cairn and left all the gear they could do without,

> ... as we must try to get along as fast as possible ... did about 11 miles—we are 99 miles from Hut Point. No improvement in Mr. Evans but worse ... I am giving him oatmeal and seal liver and meat out of the pemmican and other changes of food as we have got.

> 12th A fine day. We did about seven miles, but the surface was very heavy and dragging rather stiff for us as there is only two of us now. Mr. Evans is getting along as best he can on ski. I hope he will be able to keep on his legs. We have got to lift him on to his skis now and help him about. It is nearly come to a climax. We shall soon have to drag him.

> 14th Feb. Started this morning but had to stop and dump everything we possibly could and take Mr. Evans on the sledge. We still have 70 miles to go. No doubt we shall have our work cut out, but we must try and do our best to get to Hut Point in Safety.

That evening Lieutenant Evans was completely helpless and quite unable to stand. He ordered Lashly and Crean to leave him in his sleeping bag and to go on without him.

15th Feb. We were able to put in a good march.

17th Feb. ... we are now 30 miles from Hut Point. Mr. Evans is getting worse but we must try and get him along although it is hard slogging and we are not as strong as we might be after our pull.

18th Feb. Started to move Mr. Evans this morning but he collapsed and fainted right away. Got him round again and used last drop of brandy. Put him on the sledge after a while and got away although he is pretty bad. But found handling so heavy we decided to camp and Crean proceed on foot to Hut Point and get relief in some shape. He left here at 9 a.m.—the distance 30 miles. This being an ideal day I hope it will keep clear for Crean to reach Hut Point in safety.

The entries in Lashly's diary stopped at this point as he and Evans settled down to wait for help to arrive. After a hazardous journey alone Crean arrived at Hut Point 18 hours later at 3.30 a.m., delirious with exhaustion. Half an hour later a blizzard came down and it was not until the following afternoon that the Naval Surgeon, Edward Atkinson, was able to set out with a dog team. On finding the two men he was lost in admiration for Lashly's care and nursing of Evans.

It has been said by other writers of this expedition that there might well have been a different ending to this saga had Scott accepted the advice of Dr. Edward Wilson and Dr. Edward Atkinson and chosen 'hard-as-nails' William Lashly to accompany him on that last leg. Be that as it may, both Lashly and Crean were awarded the Albert Medal in 1913 for saving the life of Lieutenant Evans, later to achieve fame in the First World War as 'Evans of the Broke', and Flag Rank.

In 1932 William Lashly returned to Hambledon, where he built a house which he called Minna Bluff after a promontory about 50 miles south-east of Hut Point, not all that far from the spot where he and Evans waited for relief. Hanging in his hall was the harness he and Tom Crean used to tow their heavy sledge on that long haul northwards. He died in 1940 at the age of seventy-three. He was buried in Hambledon churchyard and, on his instructions, no headstone marks his grave.

47   William Lashly.

The first half of the 20th century will always be remembered for two devastating wars. The war memorial in the churchyard tells its own special story through the 33 names of Hambledon men who gave their lives in the First World War and the eight who never returned from the Second World War.

In 1939 the Hambledon Defence Volunteers, the successors of the Hambledon Volunteers of Napoleon's day, were formed. They started with about 140 men and youths, but the young men soon left to join the fighting services, and from 1940 the Home Guard, as it was then renamed, included about fifty volunteers. There were also Special Constables, an Observer Corps who manned a post on the hill towards Rushmere, Wardens and a Women's Institute canteen for the many W.R.N.S. and soldiers billeted in Hambledon. Many additional hands worked in the fields to provide the extra food so urgently needed; old common lands which had not been tilled for centuries felt the rough caress of plough and harrow. Many Hambledon families were represented in the fighting forces.

During the war about 100 high explosive and 1,000 incendiary bombs fell in the parish, mostly near the village. One house at the top of Speltham Hill was demolished, but its occupants, flying in the face of all standard advice, dashed out into the lane when they heard the bomb whistling down and so saved their lives. Hartridge's Brewery was the only other building to receive a direct hit by a German bomb and once again there were no casualties. In fact the only casualty in the village was caused by one of our own anti-aircraft shells which, failing to explode in the sky, detonated on crashing through the roof of a house.

A short while before the 1944 Normandy landings, the people of Hambledon emerged from their houses one morning to find parties of soldiers painting large, numbered rectangles along the roadsides. Their work was swiftly and efficiently done; by the same afternoon Hambledon looked like a huge games board. A few days later a stream of vehicles started passing through the village. The heavy diesel beat of the large lorries, the rumble of armoured cars, the clatter of light tanks and the roar of heavy tanks filled the air as the great armada of noisy metal monsters staged south to embarkation points for the landings on the coast of occupied France. When at last the cavalcade stopped, each rectangle was filled with a car, lorry, carrier or tank.

The village welcomed the new arrivals and did what they could for the officers and men of these vehicles parked along its streets. The welcome given by Mr. and Mrs. Hooker of West Street to the crew of the tank parked immediately outside their gate knew no bounds for, by some extraordinary coincidence, it included their son. Young Mr. Hooker of the Royal Tank Regiment said later that they had moved from Aldeburgh in Suffolk to Worthing to waterproof the tanks. There they were told that their destination was near Portsmouth, and while en route Mr. Hooker was given a numbered parking square, which, he laconically remarked, ' ... happened to be outside my parents' home, Bower Mead, Hambledon.' His wife, who lived in Waterlooville, was soon informed, and the family was united for two days, after which the visitors drove to Bury Lodge to change money into francs and thence to Stokes Bay. There they embarked into

Landing Craft (Tanks) and sailed for France from where, I am happy to report, Mr. Hooker, in due course, safely returned.

On 22 May 1944, His Majesty King George VI visited Hambledon to review his troops poised in and around the village for the invasion of Europe. It was a memorable day; not only did the entire army billeted in the vicinity turn out, but so did the entire village. The parade took place in Chestnut Meadow opposite Bury Lodge, in flawless sunshine. The men, looking immaculate, moved as if they had been practising for this parade all their lives, and Hambledon looked its best; the chestnuts in the meadow and the beeches in the hanger behind were bursting with the fresh green of new spring leaves. As the King turned to leave the parade he remarked to General Butler of Bury Lodge, who was escorting him from the meadow, 'What a beautiful setting!'

On the Sunday after the King's visit, Hambledon church was packed full, as churches in time of war, danger or disaster so often are. There must have been some four to five hundred people in the congregation, Hambledonians and soldiers, amongst whom there was a very high proportion of Welshmen. Many friendships had been made between the village and their guests who, as everyone knew, were soon to leave the comparative peace of Hambledon to fight their way across Europe. It is not difficult to imagine how charged with emotion that service was. The hymn before the sermon was:

> Oh God, our help in ages past,
> Our hope for years to come,
> Our shelter from the stormy blast,
> And our eternal home.

Not for centuries, if ever, had the old timbered roof strained to such a volume of singing. The Welshmen sang as only the Welsh can, and at the hymn's end there was scarcely a dry eye in the Hambledon pews. The vicar, the Rev. A.C. Champion, stood in the pulpit, cleared his throat noisily, and in an unusually husky voice declared, 'You sang that hymn so well we'll sing it again!' And sing it again they did. On completion of the service the organist played as the voluntary *Men of Harlech*. The Welshmen rose to a man and once again the timbered roof echoed to a volume of singing it is never likely to experience again.

The village seemed strangely quiet and empty when they left, those officers and men. Many of them are still talked about today, though there are fewer and fewer of the older Hambledonians left who remember those events of half a century ago—but no one who attended that last service will ever forget it.

Most towns and villages have their 'haunted houses' and their spectres, and some places have terrifying tales to chill the spine. Hambledon too has its ghosts—but are there really such presences? Twelfth-century Rookwood is said to be haunted by monks, while an old man in red carpet slippers is supposed to share The Hermitage with a grey lady, but no one in Hambledon today even knows anyone who has seen these phantoms. They are kept 'alive' by village legend alone, for there is not a scrap of evidence to support them. So we may dismiss the monks of Rookwood and the old man of The Hermitage, with his grey consort, and send them back to the shadows where they belong. However, there are some stories that are not so easily dismissed. The facts surrounding them are set out fairly and the actual stories are related, where possible, in the words of those who experienced them; judge them as you will.

Miss Nina Butler used to live in Hambledon with her father, Sir Thomas Butler. As her parents often visited the Charnocks who lived at Whitedale until 1912, she knew Dorothy Charnock, the daughter of the family, well. Dorothy was born at Whitedale towards the end of the last century, and late one evening in 1905 or 1906 she was in the pantry at Whitedale. Miss Butler continues her story:

> It was quite dark and the shutters were drawn across the pantry window which looked out to the front of the house. Suddenly she heard the sounds of a carriage coming up the drive and, opening the shutters, she saw what she took to be a carriage passing the pantry window. It was too dark for her to see much of the coach, but she saw the lights and heard the horses, the jingle of the harness and the sound of the wheels on gravel. As it passed out of sight she left the pantry and, wondering who it could be, opened the front door and looked out. There were no sounds, no movement, no dark silhouettes, no light; there was nothing in the drive.

The Taylors followed the Charnocks at Whitedale. Sir Thomas (known by his family and close friends as Tim) and Lady Taylor are both now dead. Dorothea Taylor lived the last seven years of her life at Harfield with her cousin, Marian Walker (alas now departed from us as well). Many times they discussed the strange story of the Whitedale coach but never a reasonable explanation could they find. Miss Walker continues the story:

48 Whitedale, *c*.1906, when the Charnocks lived there, showing the driveway where the phantom coach and horses were seen and heard on three occasions before the First World War.

Shortly before the 1914-18 war the Taylors were expecting some friends who were driving over to have dinner with them. They were waiting in the drawing room, when they heard the carriage coming up the drive. They got up to welcome their guests in the hall, but when the front door was opened, nobody was there—no coach, no horses, no coachman, no guests. The Taylors learned later that their friends had had an accident, and, though no one was badly hurt, they had been unable to complete their journey.

Some months later on a cold winter's night, my cousin, Dorothea Taylor, her husband and one or two guests who were staying in the house, were sitting round the fire in the drawing room. They had had dinner and were waiting for the coffee to be served. As the maid came in with the tray, the sounds of a carriage and horses were heard coming up the drive. Everyone looked up in surprise.

'Who on earth can that be?' said Tim Taylor.

The maid put down the tray, went into the hall, drew back the heavy curtains and opened the front door. It was a bitterly cold night and outside there was a deathly quiet—no coach, no steaming horses, no lights, no people were to be seen. These incidents have never been explained.

No one has seen or heard the spectral carriage with its phantom horses and ghostly guests since that date shortly before 1914.

Park House has an austere beauty in a gaunt, Tudor way. It stands on its own among its trees, has a priest's hide concealed in the thickness of one of its walls and manages to look as if it ought to be haunted. Mrs. Betty Seymour-Price, the daughter of a previous owner, lived at Park for many years from girlhood onwards, and loved the old house. She relates that on two occasions, about the year 1944, she clearly heard, at night, heavy footsteps descending the attic stairs in the four-storey part of the house. 'These footsteps were unmistakably clear and quite inexplicable. None of the family or servants had been anywhere near that part of the house.'

The present owner states categorically that there are no ghosts at Park. Others who have stayed there are not always in agreement but are nonetheless reluctant to discuss the subject. There has been vague talk of 'an eerie atmosphere in certain rooms', 'strange feelings' and unusual or inexplicable noises. There is one story, though, which is quite clear.

In the mid-1950s a naval family rented Park. Mrs. Barbara Dyer tells of a day a few weeks after their arrival:

It was a sunny autumn morning and I was making my young son's bed when I felt a sudden chill in the room. I looked up and saw the figure of a boy dressed in the clothes of a Cavalier, standing in the doorway. As I looked, it (or 'he') faded, leaving the impression of a boyish face with dark eyes. It was after this that Edward, my son, began screaming at night, always at the same time, and there was always the same chill pervading the room as on that first morning. There was only the feel of something or someone in the room; there was nothing to be seen.

Needless to say, we soon moved Edward into another room and had no more bother, even though several months later the room was used as a bedroom again. There is no doubt in my mind that parts of Park are haunted.

The boy Cavalier has never been seen again. Could he have been a trick of imagination, or of light and shadow? Mrs. Dyer is quite certain that he was not.

Rear Admiral and Mrs. C.D. Madden tell a rather odd story about King's Rest, known in 1800 as Brew's Bake House, and which in 1651 was the farm cottage close by the house of Thomas Symons, and the house where King Charles II spent his last night in England before his flight to France.

Mrs. Madden writes:

> One evening between eight-thirty and nine-thirty, early in October in 1947, my husband and I were sitting, as we usually did in the evening, one on either side of the fireplace in the drawing room of King's Rest, where we were living at the time. My husband was reading and I was smocking a child's dress. The far end of the room was not well lit, as the lights were concentrated on my sewing and my husband's book.
>
> We were both attracted by the sound of a latch lifting, and both looked up at the door that was opening, the door at the far end of the drawing room that opens into a small almost underground room, built into the hill. We were both surprised as nothing but some packing cases was stored there and there was no draught or current of air. Before we could say anything the room was filled with what one can only describe as the aura that sometimes attends people of *very* great charm. It was as if everyone in a room full of people was very happy.
>
> We both found ourselves standing up; I held out my hand as if to welcome a guest. The door from the drawing room to the dining room (behind the chair in which my husband had been sitting) then opened—my husband was now facing this door—and closed again. We turned to each other rather like two dogs with our hair 'on end', and covered with goose flesh though it was not cold.
>
> 'We have a visitor,' I said. 'Did you see him?' Alas neither of us saw anything but the opening doors.
>
> The next morning General Butler came down from Bury Lodge at about half past ten as he did most mornings. I asked him if he had ever seen a ghost when they were in the cottage during the war. He was at once fascinated and produced the description of the arrival of Charles II in October 1651. It all seemed to fit in curiously. I must say that though we knew why the house was called King's Rest, it had never occurred to me that he might come back. At no other time when we were there did we ever feel or see anything, but undoubtedly the house had, for us, a particularly happy atmosphere.

Seventy-five years ago Captain and Mrs. Harvey lived in 17th-century Cams, one of the loveliest houses in Hambledon. When old Mrs. Harvey died the house passed to her daughter, Mrs. Ena Dawe, and finally to her grand-daughter, Mrs. Pamela Cullingham. Before the Harveys my grandparents lived at Cams—Edward Goldsmith, weak, lazy and Protestant and Anastasia, dominant, energetic and Catholic; an ill-assorted pair to understate the case. While she was still living at Cams Mrs. Cullingham wrote:

> Early in the morning of the 22nd of December, 1922, my mother and grandmother were woken by steps coming along the passage. They stopped at my mother's door and then there was a knock. My mother was half asleep and thought it was the morning tea. The steps then moved on to my grandmother's room and again there was a knocking on the door, after which the steps moved on up the stairs to the box room and the bedroom up there. My grandmother got out of bed and looked out to see who it was when she heard the steps going up the stairs, but to her surprise there was no one to be seen. This must have been in the small hours of the morning because the

real morning tea arrived later. I can well remember the excitement and speculation at breakfast time. Later we heard that old Mr. Goldsmith had died in the early hours of that very morning.

Footsteps and inexplicable knockings have never been heard again, but we do frequently hear the voices of two people talking. These voices seem to come from the upstairs passage by the corner near the bathroom, but trying to trace the exact spot is rather like seeking the source of a rainbow. The voices are always those of a man and a woman and though they can be heard easily you can never quite make out what they are saying. Sometimes they are peaceful, sometimes happy and sometimes in heated argument. As a child I slept in a little room at the top of the back stairs and I never felt alone when they were there. Many people have heard these voices and they all say how friendly they seem, 'not a bit frightening' being the most used phrase.

There is no record of these voices in my grandparents' time, so could they have belonged to Edward and Anastasia? I wonder. They have not been heard in recent times, but the present owners of Cams say that on several occasions footsteps have been heard and describe them as a 'measured tread', often going up to the attic.

In old houses stairs creak, windows and doors make strange noises on windy nights and have the occasional knack of unfastening themselves when they are not properly secured. Certain houses have a strong atmosphere of the past, and light and shadows and imagination may combine to play tricks. Nevertheless who can refute, offhand, the phantom coach of Whitedale, the colourful little Cavalier of Park, or the singular presence at King's Rest which caused two people to get up to welcome a guest they could not see? Who can dismiss the ghostly voices of Cams heard by so many people?

Hambledon has much to look back on and much to be proud of today. Despite the lusts of the speculator and developer—some of whom have a highly developed sense of greed to match a marked lack of taste or scruple—Hambledon is still a village, and still retains its rural charm. There is a thriving Cricket Club, and an Arts Society incorporating music, drama, painting, poetry, local history and youth groups. The Horticultural Society show, held on the fourth Saturday in August, has attained a very high standard of exhibits and draws experts from a wide area of southern Hampshire. The old roundabouts with their steam organs and the boat-type swings, in which my brother always managed to be sick when his end was in the ascendant, have given way to the more manoeuvrable sideshows of today. In the evening there is a torchlight parade and the traffic on the main road through Hambledon is held back while dozens of children, their parents, grandparents and friends march through the village with their flaming brands.

Hartridge's soft drinks factory and the vineyard may be considered as Hambledon's liquid assets. In 1882 Francis Hartridge took over the Alliance Brewery from a Dr. Gammon who ran both his business and his surgery from Alliance House (now called Weaverlands). Under new and perhaps more single-minded direction the brewery prospered, and regular deliveries of ale departed from Hambledon in horse-drawn wagons. Hops and barley were also sold to local farmers who made their own beer. The mineral waters and soft drinks side of the business was started at about the turn of the century, in addition to the brewery. During the First World War many horses were requisitioned from farms and businesses for service in France and Belgium. Early in 1915 some army officers visited

Hartridge's Alliance Brewery. All the magnificent dray horses were taken out of their stables and paraded round the yard. Three of the best were chosen, and with great sadness the family and work force watched them leave. They never returned.

The brewery continued to thrive through the 1920s and '30s under Francis's sons, Edward and Austen, producing new brands of ale and quality soft drinks. Then came the terrible night in August 1940 when Hartridge's Alliance Brewery took a direct hit from a German bomb. Mercifully there were no casualties, but it was a sad sight to see so much ale flowing down the street. The brewery was damaged beyond repair and was never replaced, but the soft drinks plant was left intact, and within a few days Hartridge's trucks were again negotiating the blitzed streets of Portsmouth and Southampton.

The factory passed into the hands of Edward's son Geoffrey and on his retirement in 1988 to his three sons Geoffrey, Christopher and Martin. The company currently employs 50 people and transports its soft drinks, including bottles of crystal-clear Hambledon water, to all the southern counties from Devon to Kent, as well as to London, Birmingham and Warwick.

In 1951 Sir Guy and Lady Salisbury-Jones, more as a family hobby than anything else, planted vines in the field below their house, Mill Down, and in so doing they led the way in the revival of English wine production. There are now over 500 English

49   Hartridge's Alliance Brewery after a direct hit by a German bomb in August 1940.

vineyards. The gentle south-facing slope in front of Mill Down, the chalky soil and viticultural technology imported from the Champagne region, together with a great deal of hard work, produced an excellent dry white wine, which was sold and served throughout Britain, in many embassies abroad, on board the *QE2*, and even in France and the United States. The vineyard was open to the public and Sir Guy and Lady Salisbury-Jones welcomed several thousand visitors every year. Their 'hobby' had grown and succeeded beyond their wildest dreams, and there came a time when Sir Guy ruefully remarked '... and now the vineyard runs us.' The labels on the bottles bore the symbol of the old curved cricket bats, a happy thought that once again there was an association between Hambledon, Cricket and Wine.

In 1986 Mill Down and the vineyard changed hands. Over the next few years the number of vines was doubled; some—about two acres worth—were planted in a known frost-pocket. A large winery and underground cellar were built but, strangely, marketing activities were reduced and the property was closed to tourists. These were not happy times for English wine makers. The recession of the late '80s and early '90s bit hard and many vineyards were in danger of being submerged in the unwelcome 'wine-lakes' of France, Italy and Germany.

In 1992 the Hambledon vineyard changed hands once again, and the wine from the next two harvests was made by another winery. In 1994 most of the vines planted in the late '80s, including those unwisely placed where the frosts linger, were removed. The oldest unproductive vines were also taken out and the vineyard was restored to its 1986 size—the size it was when the Salisbury-Joneses left. The intention is to return

50   The Hambledon vineyard. The Vendange or grape harvest in late September 1960. Sir Guy is on the left wearing a hat and Lady Salisbury-Jones is fifth from the right.

to a smaller enterprise with a re-emphasis on quality and, at the time of writing, the current owners, Mr. and Mrs. Larock, are working with Sir Guy's son, Raymond, to try to bring this about.

In 1993 rumour reached the village and beyond, that the brewery, Ind Coope, was about to change the name of that famous hostelry, the *Bat and Ball Inn*. Storm clouds gathered, there were mutters of sacrilege and threats of boycott, even letters to *The Times*. In the event the name was not so much changed as modified. A large sign on one side of the old pub proclaims to all who pass, *Natterjacks at the Bat and Ball*. This linking of bat and ball with a toad of increasing rarity seems incomprehensible. But the name was chosen light-heartedly to attract a younger generation to the bar of the *Bat and Ball* and also to the large restaurant recently added to the rear of the building, which is run by 'Natterjacks'. Happily the pub thrives, probably due as much to its nostalgic connections as to its links with the *bufo calamita*.

There is one new development that has been welcomed by the village as a whole, and that is a small Housing Association estate containing four bungalows, two flats and a mixture of two- and three-bedroomed houses. It was completed in 1993, and by mid-year all the buildings were leased to Hambledon families or ex-Hambledonians. It has been named Lashly Meadow after one of the village's greater sons. Fortunately these bungalows and houses were built on rising ground, for in 1994 Hambledon suffered the worst floods the village had seen for a hundred years.

In 1896 a young girl in her teens wrote in her journal, 'Water over the road at Park. Park cellar flooded and this has never happened before.' In later years this girl was to describe to her daughter, now Mrs. Ida Barrett, how the flood waters froze and how she and her friends were able to 'skate from Park to Poore's'. Park stands at the eastern end of the village and Poore's Farm, now known as Hook Vinney, at the western end, two miles apart. In those days many cellars flooded every winter, but they all had their own outlets known as 'dip-holes', and it was essential to keep these clear. As, winter after winter, the water from the chalk downs above the valley was released through springs, it flowed from the slightly higher east end of Hambledon to the west along an open ditch beside the road. This often took on the appearance of a small river, and frequently overflowed and flooded the flinty road. It eventually passed under Cams Lane through a large culvert known to the children of the area as 'The Bunny', because in its tunnels, in dry weather, they used to play, disappearing like rabbits into a warren. Harry Lott's daughter, Ena, tells of an occasion when, as a child, she and some friends had incurred the wrath of Hambledon's Police Constable, Mr. Spreadbury. It was with good reason that they hid in The Bunny, for they knew all too well that he kept a marble in the forefinger of his glove, and when he gave them an avuncular tap on the head, it hurt. One can imagine Ena's anxiety when she heard Mr. Spreadbury on the road above them telling her father, who happened to be a Special Constable, that he knew the little blight-ers had run up Cams Lane, but he would catch them when they came down.

Later land drainage schemes helped to reduce the frequency and severity of the flooding, and the ditch finally dried up and was eventually lost altogether to highway improvements. The 'dip-holes' too were lost, as many frontages were paved over.

During the last four months of 1993 more than two and a half times the average rainfall fell over Hampshire. Between 17 December and 12 January the water table beneath Hambledon rose 60 ft., taking it above the level of the road through the village. Even if the old ditch and the dip-holes had still existed they could not possibly have coped with the deluge of water that poured off the fields onto the road and that rose beneath houses until it filled cellars, even bursting through the floors of basements that had been 'floodproofed'. Many people had installed electrical fittings in their cellars, including mains junction boxes, so there was a danger that the whole area might be cut off from electrical supplies. As the water table continued to rise there was the threat that about forty houses might become uninhabitable.

Mrs. Katharine Nisbet's house in East Street was one whose cellar was flooded. The water rose through her cellar and overflowed into her drawing room and finally into her dining room and kitchen. This rising tide was stemmed by two pumps close to the house and a fire engine outside which, with two others, was monitoring the situation in a number of houses in the immediate area. Mrs. Nisbet spent the morning of Sunday 15 January in her rather damp kitchen making marmalade. After lunch with

51   The 1994 flood. The dam across East Street.

a neighbour she returned to her house. The two pumps and the fire engine, whose hoses now came in through her garden door, were all noisily working away. That evening, at about 6 o'clock, she felt unwell. She made her way to the open garden door and saw the blurred vision of a blue uniform and yellow helmet.

'I think I'm going to pass out,' she said, and did so into the arms of Fireman Ken Guy of Eastleigh's White Watch. An ambulance was quickly called and, protesting vociferously, she was taken to Queen Alexandra Hospital, where carbon monoxide poisoning was diagnosed. The next day she had a visitor. It was Assistant Divisional Officer Kevin Butcher, the officer in charge that Sunday night, who presented her with a large bunch of flowers from the Hampshire Fire and Rescue Service.

The huge operation to control and lower the level of the water table underneath Hambledon lasted just over three weeks. A dam, constructed of sandbags, was built across the road at the east end of the village where water from the springs was gushing onto the road. Here three 'Green Goddesses', engines designed in the early 1950s to pump large quantities of water over long distances, and each capable of pumping out 1,000 gallons a minute, removed between them 4.3 million gallons a day. The water was pumped via six-inch hoses through the village along the streets where the open ditch once flowed, and out at the west end beyond Cams Corner. Six other 'Green Goddesses' were stationed at strategic points along the one mile run to maintain pressure

52 Winning the battle against flood water—the roads begin to dry out.

and boost the flow of water. At the same time a fleet of conventional, red fire engines and their crews were pumping out the cellars and wells of individual houses in danger, and this was round-the-clock work, for as soon as a cellar had been cleared to a safe level it started to refill. At the time when all fire engines, both red and green, were working to capacity, some twelve miles of hoses snaked their way alongside the roads, carrying, at the peak of the emergency, a total of over 10 million gallons a day, and the daily cost of the fuel alone amounted to £800. Thanks to the Fire Brigades from all 55 stations in Hampshire, a major disaster was averted.

***

In an earlier chapter we compared the Hambledon of the 1320 survey (which so upset Alexander, Prior of Winchester) with the Hambledon of 300 years later, as seen through the Parliamentary Survey of 1647. The 20th century marks a further 300-year step. It is difficult to contemplate what the next 300-year leap will bring to the village by 2247. Will our descendants, if they survive the step at all, conceivably be able to imagine the rolling downs and fields, the vast forests and much used Christian church of Saxon Hamelanduna, with a population not yet in three figures?

What perils await them? Will they be pawns of continental bureaucracy or will they be softened out of existence by a welfare state whose cornucopia may one day cease to flow? Will they survive the twin spectres of World Famine and World War? It has been said that these are changing times, but 'winds of change' have blown through Hambledon before, as when the Romans left the villa to the plundering Jutes and Saxons, when new Norman overlords first came, when Richard I drained the country of money to pay for his Crusade, when the Black Death swept through the village, when the Church of England broke away from Rome, when Cromwell's major generals cut down the maypoles, when war and revolution threatened—but Hambledon lives on. People come and people go, and their passing is like a fleeting shadow, and yet this myriad procession of human beings is the lifeblood of our village, whose story is the sum total of all their lives.

Bibliography

Altham, H.F. and Swanton, E.W., *A History of Cricket*, 4th edition, 1948

Arlott, John (ed.),*From Hambledon to Lords. The Classics of Cricket*, 1948

Ashley-Cooper, F.S., *The Hambledon Cricket Chronicle*, 1924

Bryant, Arthur, (ed.), *The Letters of Charles II,* 1935

Capes, W.W., *Bishops of Winchester*, 1907

Churchill, W., *History of the English Speaking Peoples*, Vols. I-IV, 1956-8

Cobbett, William, ed. G.D.H. and M. Cole, *Rural Rides*, 1930

Ellis, A.R., *Under Scott's Command*, 1969

Fea, Allan, *The Flight of the King*, 1897

Godwin, G.N., *The Civil War in Hampshire*, 1904

Goldsmith, Dora, *Hambledon Past and Present*, 1909

Goodman, A.F., *Winchester Cathedral Cartulary*, 1927

Hampshire Chronicle, 23 August 1782 and 10 March 1783

Hampshire Field Club Papers and Proceedings

Hampshire Record Society, 3 vols. 1889 to 1894

Hawkes, J. and C., *Prehistoric Britain*, 1943

Haygarth, A., *Scores and Biographies*, 1895

Heyer, Georgette, *Royal Escape*, 1938

Heysham, W.N. (*Aesop*), *Sporting Reminiscences of Hampshire*, 1864

Hope, J.F.R., *A History of Hunting in Hampshire*, 1950

Knight, R., *Hambledon's Cricket Glory*, Vols. 3-12, 1976-93

Lucas, E.V., *The Hambledon Men*, 1907

Muir, R., *British History*, 1929

Norman, Terry, *Hambledon and Denmead, A Photographic History*, 1976

Norman, Terry, *Journeys to Yesterday*, 1979

Read, D.H. Moutray, *The Highways and Byeways in Hampshire*, 1908

Swanton, E.W., (ed.), *The World of Cricket*, 1967

Thorpe, James, *Cricket Bag*, 1929

Trevelyan, G.M., *History of England*, 3rd edition, 1945

Victoria County History, Hampshire, 1900-14

Vinogradoff, P., *Oxford Studies in Social and Legal History*, Vol. V., 1909

Warner, R., *Collections for the History of Hampshire*, 1795

Warner, R., *Hampshire Section of Domesday Book*, 1789

Birch's *Cartularium Saxonicum*
Kemble's *Codex Diplomaticus*
Registers of John Sandall 1316-1319 and Reginald Asser 1320-1323
Register of Bishop Orton, 1333-1345
Register of William of Wykeham, 1376
Calendar of Patent Rolls, Edward III, 1327-1330
Calendar of State Papers, Vol. VIII 26 Henry VIII, 1535
Calendar of State Papers Domestic, Vol. XXVIII
Abbreviatio Rotulorum Originalium, published 1810
The Narrative of Colonel Gounter of Racton, 'as it was taken from his mouth by a person of worth a little before his death', *c*.1655

Index

Figures in bold refer to illustrations

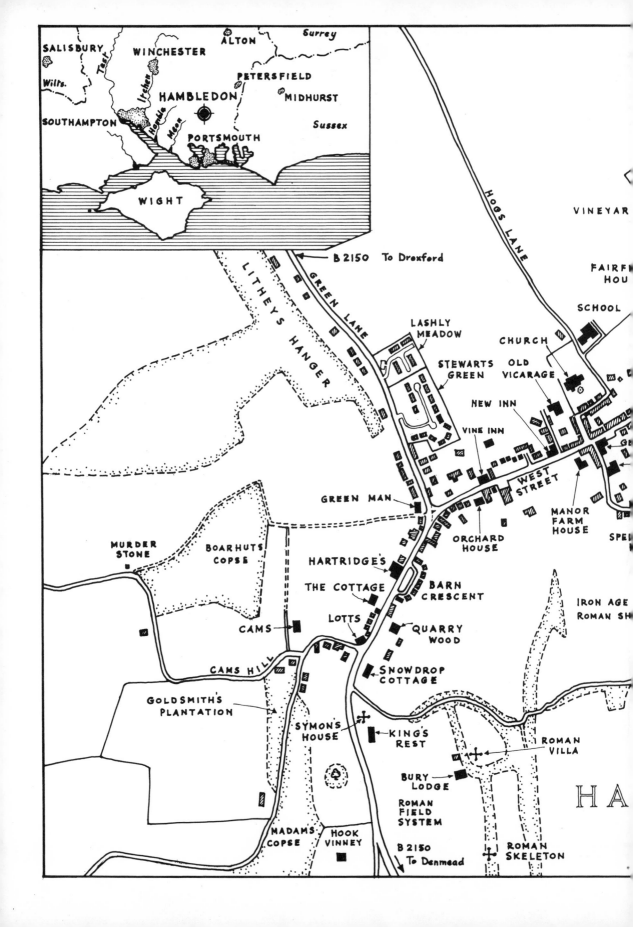